The
Depressed
Child

A Parent's Guide for Rescuing Kids

The
Depressed
Child

A Parent's Guide for Rescuing Kids

DR. DOUGLAS A. RILEY

Taylor Trade Publishing

Dallas, Texas

Published by Taylor Publishing Company
1550 West Mockingbird Lane
Dallas, Texas 75235
www.taylorpub.com

Library of Congress Cataloging-in-Publication Data

Riley, Douglas.
   The depressed child : a parent's guide for rescuing kids /
Douglas A. Riley.
      p. cm.
   ISBN 0-87833-187-5 (PBK.)
   1. Depression in children—Popular works. 2. Depression in
adolescence—Popular works. 3. Cognitive therapy for children.
4. Cognitive therapy for teenagers. I. Title.

RJ506.D4 R54 2001
618.92'8527—dc21   00-062033

10 9 8 7 6 5 4 3 2 1

Printed in the United States of America

For Debra, Collin, and Sam

Contents

 *Acknowledgments*

No psychologist can write convincingly about children and teenagers without having learned from others. I am pleased to take the opportunity to publicly thank the people I have learned from in the past and continue to learn from today.

The Department of Counselor Education and Counseling Psychology at Western Michigan University supported me throughout my graduate education with grants and assistantships. I remain grateful to the department, and I hope this book reflects positively on its faculty and staff.

While at Western Michigan, I had the opportunity to study with Dr. Edward Trembley, who has spent much of his professional career pondering just how depression works. It is thanks to him that I am aware that depression is much more than a biochemical imbalance. Dr. Trembley continues to have much to say about how depression affects a person's sense of who they are, how they view the world and others around them, and how hopeful they remain about the future.

My mentor and committee chairman, Dr. Robert Betz, was instrumental in helping me understand the power of having children, teenagers, and adults think about how they think. Much of my insistence that we must examine our own "internal program" before we can make meaningful change is due to his influence.

I am particularly indebted to a number of pediatricians in the Newport News, Virginia, area who are supportive of my work, and with whom I have the enjoyable opportunity to discuss cases not only from a psychological viewpoint, but from a medical viewpoint as well. I wish to thank the physicians, nurses, and staff members at the Children's Clinic, Peninsula Pediatrics, and Newport News Pediatrics for their referrals.

Camile Cline and Maura Keese, my editors at Taylor Trade Publishing, have worked diligently to provide me with detailed feedback throughout all phases of this project. While the mistakes and shortcomings in this book are most certainly mine, their thoughtful comments have certainly helped shape it into its final form.

I continue to be flattered that parents seek out my counsel and allow me to work with their children. In this regard I must thank them for the trust that they have extended to me.

Finally, this book could not have been completed without the help and support of my wife, Debra Lintz-Riley. She has listened to and discussed my thoughts and ideas on probably more occasions than she wished, and I am deeply in her debt.

The Depressed Child

A *Parent's Guide for Rescuing Kids*

Introduction

The Purpose of Depression

What is depression for?

On the surface of it, this sounds like a crazy question. What is depression *for*? The gut response would be that it is not *for* anything. It serves no purpose, other than making its host miserable. It is a disease, an illness, a syndrome to be eradicated. There is no *for*.

Don't dismiss the question too quickly. After all, there was a time in history when people might have asked what fevers or pain were for and scoffed at the notion that they served any medical purpose in helping to understand what was going on in the body. It seems unlikely, once you think about it, that a mental state as complicated and miserable as depression happens for no reason at all.

• • •

The symptoms of a Major Depressive Episode, according to the *Diagnostic and Statistical Manual of Mental Disorders*, fourth edition (American Psychiatric Association, 1994), can be drastic:

- Depressed mood most of the day, nearly every day, as

indicated by either subjective report (for example, feeling
sad or empty) or observation made by others. In children
and adolescents, can be irritable mood.

- Markedly diminished interest or pleasure in all, or almost
  all, activities most of the day, nearly every day.
- Significant weight loss when not dieting or weight gain
  (that is, a change of more than five percent of body weight
  in a month).
- Insomnia or hypersomnia nearly every day.
- Psychomotor agitation or retardation nearly every day.
- Fatigue or loss of energy nearly every day.
- Feelings of worthlessness or excessive or inappropriate
  guilt nearly every day.
- Diminished ability to think or concentrate, or
  indecisiveness, nearly every day.
- Recurrent thoughts of death, recurrent suicidal ideation
  without a specific plan, formulation of a specific plan for
  committing suicide, or a suicide attempt.*

In order to receive a diagnosis of Major Depressive Episode, a
child must show five or more of the symptoms in a two-week period, and these must represent a change from previous functioning.
Between three and six percent of children in the population may
experience these symptoms.

While such a symptom list is useful in alerting us to the existence of depressive symptoms in children and adolescents, it falls
far short of helping us to understand what causes depression and
what we can do about it. Depression, I believe, is best understood
when not viewed solely as an illness or as a set of symptoms, but as
a message.

• • •

*Reprinted with permission from the *Diagnostic and Statistical Manual of Mental
Disorders*, Fourth Edition. Copyright 1994 American Psychiatric Association.

The position taken in this book is that childhood and adolescent depression is a feedback loop, the brain's attempt to get the conscious mind's attention. The message of depression is not always easy to hear or easy to accept. What it is trying to tell you is that something in your life must change before you can feel better.

Depression gives you feedback about three aspects of your life, any of which might require change in order for you to feel better. The first of these aspects, and probably the most well known these days, is biochemistry. The second is environmental stress. The third possible cause of depression is your own thoughts and beliefs.

The American public has become impressively educated to the fact that mood can be drastically affected by hormones and neurotransmitters. It is not at all uncommon for parents to telephone my office and say that they think their child might have a "chemical imbalance."

Our understanding that chemical imbalances can cause depression has left us with a tendency to forget about other factors. External stressors, such as too much work, failure at an important project, loss of a relationship, or too much arguing and tension at home, can create terrible mood states. Internal events, such as what someone thinks or believes about themselves, can lead to depression. To make matters even more complex, chemistry interacts with stress, stress interacts with thinking, thinking interacts with chemistry, and so on, until the head begins to spin.

HOPELESS BELIEFS

This book focuses primarily on the third cause of depression in children and adolescents, the form of depression that I refer to as "cognitive depression" because it is caused by one's own thoughts and beliefs. Why the focus on thoughts and beliefs? For two reasons. First, negative thoughts about themselves and their lives almost always accompany depression in children and adolescents. Second, when we help these same children and adolescents modify what they think and believe about themselves, they almost always report that they feel better.

Think of it like this: The brain is an organic computer of sorts. Thoughts and beliefs are its software. If, for example, the main computer at your place of employment begins to add three plus four to get six, chances are someone in the information systems department will be staying up late. We should be equally alarmed when we hear our children voice the remarkably hopeless beliefs about themselves which act as fuel for depression, beliefs such as "I'm no good" or "I'm so stupid." We should be no less vigilant in our attempt to fix how our children think than we would be in fixing how our office computer computes.

Fortunately, the brain can be reprogrammed. But first, you have to know what the depression-causing beliefs are. Experience has taught me that the majority of depressed children and adolescents secretly believe one or more of the following ten hopeless beliefs:

Hopeless Belief #1: Death is an option.

The mind of the depressed child or adolescent can become so dominated by one or more of the beliefs described here that their combined weight becomes sufficient to shatter her desire to live. In general, a wish to die does not appear until one or more of these beliefs begin to dominate the thinking process. It is at this point that the child may come to believe that dying is a realistic option to end the negative feelings.

Hopeless Belief #2: I am made of inferior stuff.

Depressed children and adolescents frequently have a sense that others are somehow better than they are or have more inherent worth. This belief, as we shall see in almost everything associated with depression, does not have to be based in reality. It is entirely possible that the child or teenager who secretly believes that he is made of inferior stuff is smarter and more talented than almost all of his peers. When you observe a child who thinks this way interacting with his peers, you will notice that he yields easily in an argument or discussion and is often more concerned with making everyone happy than with stating his own true opinions and beliefs. Such children find it hard to stand up for themselves, even when they know clearly that others are wrong.

Hopeless Belief #3: My mistakes are proof That I am worthless.

Children and adolescents who believe this are constantly worried that they will do something wrong, and they view their mistakes as proof that there is something wrong with them. As you might guess, they also tend to view their mistakes as constituting proof that they are inferior to others, even though others are making exactly the same mistakes. Because they have little ability to accept their own fallibility, they are prone to outbursts and tantrums when they make mistakes. It goes without saying that they are also prone to blame their mistakes on others.

Hopeless Belief #4: No one will ever like me.

Perhaps because they see themselves in such a negative light, it is natural for depressed children and adolescents to believe that no one could actually like them. While they may be perfectly likable children, capable of displaying all of the social and interpersonal behaviors that are typically associated with interpersonal competence, children who believe that no one will ever like them tend to hang out on the fringes of groups. They really do want to be invited into the group but fear rejection should they be bold enough to knock on the door and announce their presence. Because of their hanging back and acting shy, others avoid them or simply fail to notice them. The depressed child or adolescent, however, interprets this in exactly the opposite way. He comes to the conclusion that he is not being invited to join the group because he is not worth liking. The kicker is that if others do act as if they like him, he turns it around and thinks: "If they really knew me, they wouldn't like me."

Hopeless Belief #5: You must be fair to me.

Just because the depressed child or adolescent believes that she is inferior or unlikable does not mean that she is not dying to be liked by others. One of the methods that depressed children use to try to get others to like them is to try to become the world's nicest person. Children locked in this role often go out of their way to make sure that they are nice to others, even when others are acting like barbarians. When the barbarians refuse to act in a way that is equally fair, depressed children become even more depressed. Nice children and adolescents fail to be assertive, even when they know it would be appropriate. They consistently shy away from confrontation.

Hopeless Belief #6: I can't live without this person.

This idea holds particularly true for the depressed adolescent. After spending a lifetime disliking himself, when someone comes along and shows an interest, sometimes just a tiny interest, the depressed adolescent often leaps to the conclusions that love has finally arrived and that it will never come again should this chance be lost. Most adolescent relationships are doomed to fail because of a depressed partner's clinging and need for constant reassurance. When relationships fail, the depressed teen often comes to believe that life is not worth living.

Hopeless Belief #7: I must be going crazy.

Every year I meet a small number of children who eventually admit to me that there seems to be a voice in their head telling them to do dangerous, harmful things to themselves or others. The voice does not sound like their own voice, and it seems to have a life of its own. They feel invaded by an alien presence, and believe that they have gone crazy. Their fears about being crazy cause them to keep this frightening phenomenon a secret from everyone.

Hopeless Belief #8: My parents didn't love me enough.

Depression can have many causes. However, over the years I have been struck by the number of depressed adults who report that they had a parent who was emotionally or physically unavailable, for whatever reason. This unavailability can be caused by the parent being forced, out of economic reality, to work too many hours or to travel too much. It can be caused by substance abuse on the part of the parent. (You can't be involved with a substance and a child at the same time, regardless of your good intentions.) It can be caused by serious parental mental illness. It can be caused by depression itself, a cycle in which depression in the parent begets depression in the child.

Hopeless Belief #9: Substances will make me happy.

Depressed adolescents are at particular risk of turning to any number of substances. They use certain substances—food, sugared drinks, candy, junk food—to soothe themselves during periods of emotional unrest. They use other substances—alcohol, marijuana, and other street drugs—to medicate themselves into either a temporary oblivion or a temporary euphoria, to help them ignore what they feel inside.

Hopeless Belief #10: Nothing will ever change.

Having read through the first nine hopeless beliefs, you can see why a depressed child or adolescent can become demoralized and begin to believe that he will never find his way out of what he is feeling. His sense of hope about the future begins to fade, and life begins to feel flat and uninteresting.

• • •

These are the beliefs that lead to cognitive depression. We will go into each of them in considerable detail in the following chapters. Keep in mind that in order to rescue your child from cognitive depression, you have to help him understand that the way he is thinking is what is actually causing him to be depressed. In order to help him escape depression, we will have to show him, sometimes quite dramatically, that his thinking is faulty. We move now to the techniques you can use to rescue your child.

Chapter 1

Planning the Rescue Mission

In order to rescue your child or adolescent from depression, you must be willing to act in a decisive manner. For children and adolescents, the depressive state makes them feel like astronauts whose tethers have been cut, and they are drifting in space. Depressed children and adolescents have the same sense of isolation and helplessness. They need someone to take charge and come to their rescue.

Taking charge requires that parents become educated on the mechanics of cognitive depression, come to understand how it works, and put together a strategy to attack and disrupt the illogical and irrational ideas that underlie cognitive depression and wreck the moods and confidence of good children and adolescents. Our attempt will be to throw a monkey wrench into cognitive depression's machinery so that all its gears and belts and spindles come to a screeching halt. In order to achieve this, there are several things that are absolutely necessary for parents to think about.

- Any successful attack on cognitive depression requires that we learn how to examine structure. Structure is composed of all of the rules, regulations, rewards, punishments, love, and nurturing which make a child or teenager feel safe and secure. The way families live together and interact can make a child feel healthy and whole, or sad and depressed.

- Remaining depressed requires that the depressed individual find "proof" that the bad things he thinks about himself or about his life are true. Without proof, depression goes away.
- Depressed children and teenagers unwittingly employ a double standard in which they accept their faults and mistakes as constituting proof of their worthlessness, yet deny that similar faults and mistakes in others means anything negative about them. They are unlikely to escape depression as long as they employ double standards in their thinking.
- As a parent, you are unlikely to help your child escape cognitive depression unless you talk to her. You will find, though, that before you can talk effectively, you must understand how to listen.

No one, least of all me, has come to such a clear understanding of how depression works that we can dust off our hands and walk away, saying to ourselves, "OK, done with that one. Let's move on to some new mystery." But my experience in working with depressed children and adolescents has taught me that if you pay attention to the type of environment a child is being raised in, listen closely to what he believes about himself, help him learn not to be more critical of himself than he would be of others, and learn to listen to him, you can go a long way in helping him feel better.

THE ISSUE OF STRUCTURE

There is a story that I told in my book, *The Defiant Child*, that is particularly germane to depressed children and adolescents. Early in my career, I spent a session working with a child, and a week later I got a phone call from his teacher. She told me that the work I was doing with him was having a marvelous effect and that I should keep it up. I thanked her for her kind comments, without telling her that having seen this boy only once, I had likely done little more than say hello and establish a friendly connection with him. The truth was that I had no idea what I had done that had been so helpful.

About a year later, I had a similar call from another teacher, about another child. The situation otherwise was the same. I had no idea what I had done that had such an impact upon the child. But this time I was determined to find out. After puzzling about it, it hit me that there was nothing that I, myself, had done that was particularly helpful to these children after just one session. What had been so helpful was that these two sets of parents, by taking the time and effort to bring their children to see me, had sent a strong, formal message to their children that they were clearly aware that something was wrong and that they intended to do something about it. There is something profoundly reassuring to a child when a parent sends a message that says, "I am the parent. I am in charge. I will do whatever is necessary to help you feel better."

I refer to this process of taking charge as "placing structure around your child." This process, as noted above, is characterized by letting the child know that, as the parent, you are aware that she is not feeling good and that you will do everything possible to help resolve the issues she faces. Over the years I have found that sending this message almost always results in a decrease in depressive symptoms, because it helps to restore the child's or teenager's sense of hope about feeling better.

Letting your child or teenager know that you are aware of how she is feeling and that you intend to talk with her, help her, and seek professional help when necessary also serves a second, somewhat more theoretical purpose. It helps to reduce uncertainty and ambiguity.

If you have known depressed children or adolescents, or if you were one yourself, you clearly understand that to them the world feels like a very uncertain, very unpredictable place. This uncertainty and unpredictability sometimes makes the world seem harsh and gives rise to a sense of hopelessness about ever feeling better. While some depressed children tolerate the unknown quite well, some don't. There is a whole group of them who cannot cope with unexpected changes or events because they feel as though they are already struggling hard enough to keep their heads above water. Unexpected changes and events are to these children the emotional equivalent of walking around a bend in the sidewalk and finding a large dog standing there growling, ready to attack.

One of the first pieces of advice I give to the parents of a depressed child or adolescent is to move quickly, using two techniques designed to drop structure down around their child. First, make sure that you close the physical distance between you and your child. It might seem quite clear to you that a depressed preadolescent will feel soothed and safe if you take the time to get her pulled up close to you on a couch while you talk to her and rub her head or tickle her arm to let her know that you intend to do whatever needs to be done to make her feel better. You might be quite surprised how soothing this will also be to your hulking adolescent boy. Remember, the depressed child's or adolescent's feelings of loneliness and isolation make him hesitant to ask for physical contact. You must make the first move.

The second thing I instruct parents to do for their depressed child or adolescent is to explain repeatedly what's going to happen, when it is going to happen, who will be there, why it's going to happen, and so on. While this may sound silly, the reason for doing this is to reduce the child's sense of uncertainty, ambiguity, and unknown. I ask parents to tell their depressed child what, why, when, where, who, and so on, until their child looks at them and says, "Mom, stop! You've already told me all of that." When your child says this to you, it means that her internal road map for the day has all of the necessary detail filled in and that she is no longer bothered by uncertainty.

• • •

As the parent, you have to make an honest determination of whether or not something you are doing is causing your child to become depressed or making her more depressed than she already is. This is not a question for the faint of heart or for the highly defensive parent. It is, however, an absolutely necessary part of making sure that the structure around your child is safe and secure enough to keep her functioning healthfully. It does little good to ask a child to examine or change the way she thinks about herself when the underlying home structure around her is not healthy.

There are several additional structural problems that can lead to potent forms of depression: patterns in which the parents argue too much, filling the home with conflict and tension; patterns in which one, if not both parents are physically or emotionally absent; patterns in which the parents are too involved with substances; and patterns in which a parent, or both parents, are physically, sexually, or emotionally abusive. Parents engaged in any of these behaviors should first look to themselves as the cause of their child's depression and should put off pursuing remedies for the child until after they modify their own behavior. Examples of the impact of structural problems upon children follow.

Attitude Boy

I see the negative effect of structural problems in my office every day. Julian, whom I refer to privately as Attitude Boy, AB for short, is sullen as only a fourteen-year-old with street smarts can be. Once a good student, helpful to his mother and liked by his neighbors, he has taken to dressing like a thug, refusing to make eye contact, and shrugging silently when asked a question. His mother brought him to see me because he has become sad, angry, and overly touchy. He is particularly this way whenever he returns from visitation with his father, who five years earlier left Julian's mother, remarried, and started a new family.

Julian's dad used to visit often. A new marriage, young stepchildren, and a new child of his own have made his visits not only less frequent, but brief. When Julian visits his dad on alternate weekends, he ends up baby-sitting for hours.

To anyone standing on the outside of this situation, it is clear that AB feels rejected, unloved, and abandoned. From everything that I can see, his decline began once his father began to lose contact with him. Julian stands little chance of getting better until his father begins to spend some serious time with him. He is fortunate in that his mother demanded that her ex-husband meet with her at my office—something some parents simply cannot bring themselves to do—to talk about their son. He is doubly fortunate that his father is listening closely and has made a promise to give him more individual time.

The Linebacker

Brian, the high school linebacker, originally came to see me because he had told his mother that he was having thoughts about killing himself. She told me that all of his life he had been quiet and reserved but popular with his peers and academically capable.

I found Brian to be politely quiet, not particularly introspective, and resistant to my attempts to find out how he felt and thought. Over time, I would often finish our sessions wondering what it was that I was missing or not doing correctly, because I found it impossible to pierce his reserve. I had come almost to the point of deciding to say to him that perhaps I should refer him to one of my colleagues, because it didn't seem that we were really engaging in any meaningful work. Before I could say that, how-ever, he said to me one day that he had finally decided to talk.

I asked him why. His response was that he had been testing me, waiting to see when I would become mad and confrontational with him or yell at him for some reason. When this did not hap-pened, he finally decided that I was safe. As you might guess, he lived in a home in which his parents bickered, fought, and yelled constantly, openly, and apparently very loudly. Brian had lost all trust in adults due to living in such an emotional pressure cooker, and he had come to believe that this lifestyle was what becoming an adult was all about. That he was depressed should come as no surprise.

Brian has done much better since his parents came in to talk and admitted to themselves that their arguing was having a de-structive impact not only on Brian, but on their entire family. They agreed, rightfully, that things had to change and that they had to begin their own process of marriage therapy in order to set things right.

The Secret Keeper

Even more distrustful of adults than the linebacker is Allison, who kept a bad secret for too long. She had been placed in a psy-chiatric hospital because she had come to believe that life was not worth living and was having serious thoughts about hurting herself.

All of this was related to the fact that an adult male friend of the family was touching her sexually whenever her parents were out of the room and he was alone with her. As with most victims, this violation of the structural boundary that should exist between children and adults totally destroyed her sense of safety. Like most victims, she began to believe that she was dirty and worthless be-cause of what had happened. These thoughts of being dirty and worthless began to dominate her thinking to the point that she could not concentrate on anything else. Her academic performance declined sharply, and she lost interest in the things that teenage girls like to do. All she wanted to do was stay home in her bedroom, the only safe place she knew.

She is relieved that everything is now out in the open. Her mother does a marvelous job of making protective physical contact with her, which is helping her to feel safe again. We continue to work hard to reprogram how she thinks about herself. She has begun to reject the idea that what this man did to her could make her dirty and worthless, which has made her feel better. Her story illustrates in the worst possible way, however, what happens to children and teenagers when adults approach them as predators.

The Five-Year-Old Crack Expert

Ariel, age five, draws pictures of her biological mother smoking a crack pipe. She draws the same picture over and over, the only difference being that sometimes it is only her mother who is smoking and sometimes it is her mother with friends.

She was initially brought to see me because she rarely talked, refused to interact with other children at kindergarten, clung to her stepmother when being dropped off at school, and had nightmares. In her nightmares her biological mother had kidnapped her and was driving away with her to a place where her father would never be able to find her.

Ariel is another of those cases in which the improvement after just several sessions was so strong that the father and stepmother were almost overly thankful for the help I was giving her. She now babbles away like a happy five-year-old should, and she interacts well with her peers at school. She impresses others as bright and happy. I have explained to the father and stepmother that while I get along well with their daughter and interact with her in ways that she enjoys, her change is due to the fact that they, as parents, have let her know that they intend to protect her at all costs.

• • •

Cases like the ones just discussed can make your hair stand on end, and rightfully so. At the same time, parents should not conclude that if they are doing something to make their child depressed, it automatically means that they are bad parents or failed parents. Parents need to keep in mind that there are sins of commission and sins of omission. I have met any number of perfectly good parents who spent too much time at the office out of the need to be good providers, only to learn that their absence had a depressing effect upon their child. I have met parents who were vastly too overbearing, but who were being so out of a desire to help their children avoid the same mistakes that the parents had made in their own young lives. It is the good parents who recognize that they are having a negative effect on their child and work hard to correct it.

THE NOTION OF "PROOF"

Once you understand that thoughts like the "hopeless beliefs" presented in the introduction dominate depressed children's thinking, it becomes obvious why they feel so bad, why they give up so easily, why they don't enjoy life, and why they can seem so irritable and explosive. If you believed the things about yourself and your life that most depressed children and adolescents believe, you would feel pretty rotten too. But why is it so difficult for depressed children and adolescents to give up the negative things they think about themselves? In order to understand this, and in order to understand where you begin your attack on the depression that is gripping your child, you have to understand the notion of "proof."

It would be difficult for a child to descend into the state of self-hatred, sadness, or inability to enjoy anything that is so often characteristic of depression without believing something that is almost impossibly negative about herself or her life. It is the impossibility and the exaggerated quality of the negative thinking that sets depressed thinking apart from simply being aware of a negative trait in one's self. Someone who has gotten a bad grade on a major test at school but is facing it in a nondepressed way might think to herself, "I've got some catching up to do." The depressed person will be much more likely to think, "I am so stupid. I'll never get into a good college. My life is wrecked."

Most of us realize that it makes no sense to believe in something that is not true, especially if believing it causes you to be depressed. But if you could tap into the brain of a depressed child to eavesdrop, you would be likely to hear a constant, nagging interior voice telling her that her mistakes and faults are unforgivable, or that she is hideous compared to her peers, or that she is just plain stupid. Her actual proof that these negative things she believes about herself are true may come solely from the fact that she believes them. *If I think I am dumb, it must be so.*

Don't let the fact that her proof is no more substantial than thin air fool you. More than one child or adolescent has killed herself over some negative belief about herself that no objective observer would agree with. It is as if her negative beliefs about herself become some sort of fuel, and at some point in time when the pressure is at its greatest it ignites into a flame that begins to consume her interior. Negative beliefs can burn quietly away until your child becomes an empty shell of her former self.

When I work with a depressed child and come to believe that he is harboring negative ideas about himself, my first move is to simply ask the child how he feels about himself. While this is a very simple question, sometimes it yields remarkable results. Children will often tell you, after you take the time to ask, that they do not feel good about themselves, or that they have not been feeling good about themselves lately, or some variation on that theme.

I then ask the child why he is not feeling good about himself. Often his reason may be that he is having trouble at school, or is in conflict with his parents or siblings, or is being picked on by his peers. When a child gives you an external source for his psychological pain, such as those just noted, your next move is to ask how, for example, being picked on by others is making him think and feel about himself. This is a vital issue. If the picking, for example, is making him believe that he is a social reject, he is likely to continue to believe this long after the picking is over and done with. It may become the way he will always think about himself.

Often, when you ask a child what he is thinking about himself, you will get an answer of "I don't know." Lots of times this is the true answer. Children and teenagers have powerful feelings and emotions which they have difficulty translating into verbal terms. We have to help them make the translation so that we can show them how to escape the bad feelings that have captured them. You help them translate by taking guesses. For example:

> ME: "What does getting picked on at school make you think about yourself?"
>
> CHILD: "I don't know."
>
> ME: "Lots of times when kids are getting picked on, they start to believe bad things about themselves. They start to think that they are rejects or that nobody will ever like them."
>
> CHILD: "I don't think anybody will ever like me."

At this point, you have unearthed the hopeless belief that is quietly eating this child alive. Think about it. If your mental program is repeating to you at the deepest level, "Nobody will ever like me, nobody will ever like me, nobody will ever like me," you are bound to end up depressed.

Once you uncover the hopeless belief, you want to keep it simple. You ask your child something like, "Do you really believe it, if you stop to think about it? Do you really believe that no one will ever like you?"

You never know what a child will say at this juncture. Some children will walk around privately thinking and believing that no one will ever like them. This can have a drastic effect on their mood and on how they interact with others. But when faced with saying out loud that they truly believe that no one will ever like them, that they are an unlikable person, they will begin to back off of the idea. This is exactly what you want. You want the child to see that such ideas are faulty, and you want him to begin to replace these faulty ideas with more realistic thinking. It will virtually doom him to walk around believing that no one will ever like him. He has ample room to escape depression when his thinking changes to understanding that while he is having trouble with his peers, he can find a way to fix anything that he might be doing wrong and can learn to ignore people who pick on him because their version of fun is to make others feel bad about themselves.

I wish it were always this simple. Often you will find that depressed children and teenagers who harbor hopeless beliefs about themselves are unwilling to give them up. In these cases, your goal is to find out what kind of proof they have that the negative idea is actually true. By asking for proof, you want them to come to the conclusion on their own that they are believing something negative about themselves in the absence of proof. The logic process then helps them to realize that it makes no sense to believe something that has no proof. This will make it easier for them to replace their "hopeless beliefs" with ideas about themselves which are grounded in reality. As a parent, you must insist to your child or teenager that what he believes about himself be realistic, both when it comes to admitting faults and acknowledging strengths.

There are two stories that I enjoy telling children and adolescents who are believing negative things about themselves in the absence of proof, and I encourage parents to tell their children stories from their own lives of a similar nature when it would be helpful. First I tell them about the man I saw at my office a number of years ago who told me that he could levitate. He complained that the top of his head was sore because he kept bumping into the ceiling. I said to him that I would like to see him levitate. He told me that it would not be possible with me watching. I told him that I had a video camera he could borrow and that he could tape himself floating upward. Again, he replied that it would not be possible to levitate under those conditions. Essentially what I was saying to him was that I wanted to see, in a tangible way, the real proof of his claim. If a child tells me that no one likes her, I want the real proof. The fact that she believes it to be true is not sufficient.

I also tell children and adolescents about the lady who told me that she could make it thunder. As with the man who claimed to be able to levitate, I told her that I wanted to see her do it. I asked her to come to my office on a day when it was not cloudy and to stand outside in the parking lot with me and whip up some thunderheads. Like the man who claimed to float, she declined my offer. Given that neither one could provide me with real evidence of their powers, I was unable to believe them. As with these two individuals, I explain to the children and adolescents I work with that if they are thinking and believing negative things about themselves, I need substantial proof in order to believe it.

There are, of course, times when a child or adolescent does give you substantial proof that he is failing to be the type of person we would hope for him to be. If a child comes to my office and tells me that he has a pattern of beating up other children and that he feels bad about it, my main reply is that I am proud of him for being willing to admit that he is doing something wrong. I tell him that I will be even prouder of him if he decides to change his behavior. We then engage in a discussion about how it is entirely appropriate for him to feel bad about himself as long as he is engaged in such behavior and that his negative feelings of guilt and shame are his mind's message telling him that change is necessary. We talk about how he probably can't really begin to feel like a truly good person until he changes his aggressive behaviors, and we discuss how people who engage in such behavior, but still feel good about themselves, have the type of brain that is willing to fool itself.

These types of talks with children and adolescents who display marked negative behavior are, sad to say, relatively rare. Most overly aggressive or sneaky or just downright mean individuals do not think that they are doing anything wrong. Fortunately, most depressed children and adolescents do not have a true mean streak. They are too often just the opposite—too nice to others or too willing to try to make others happy. When they lash out it is usually out of pain and frustration, not out of a real desire to harm others for their own entertainment.

It is important to remember that when children and teenagers venture to tell you the negative things they believe about themselves, they, from their own perspective, are taking the risk of having these things confirmed. This possibility makes them feel heavy, in an existential sense. They are dying for someone to help make their life feel light. You must go searching for proof with lightness and humor, because doing it this way sends a message to the child that it is clearly better for her to stop believing the negative things about herself which were weighing her down and making her feel rotten, but which were not grounded in reality to begin with. This is why I quickly say to children and teenagers, in a way that conveys humor and lightness, that I am not willing to simply accept their hopeless beliefs. I tell them that I demand *real* proof. To return to the girl who thought she would be a failure because she got a bad grade on an exam, the talk might go like this:

TEEN: "I got a D on my biology exam. Now I'll never get into a good college."

ME: "Do you really believe that one bad grade will keep you out of a good school?"

TEEN: "Yes. They make it too hard to get in today."

ME: "I know it's harder now than ever. But I don't think one bad grade will keep you from going to a good school."

TEEN: "Yes it will."

ME (realizing that she is stuck in her logic): "Well then, you'll have to prove to me that you are right. That's the only way I'll be willing to believe you."

TEEN: "What do you mean?"

ME: "If you can supply me proof that your grades are so bad that you can't get into any good colleges, I'll believe you. Take Michigan State for example. Michigan State is a pretty good college."

TEEN: "I agree."

ME: "They have about fifty-five thousand students there. The place is huge."

TEEN: "That's really big."

ME: "Probably not one of the fifty-five thousand students there ever got a D on a test in high school. Not even one, out of fifty-five thousand. Imagine!"

TEEN: "You're making fun of me."

ME: "No I'm not. You're the one who said getting one bad grade would prevent you from going to a good college."

TEEN: "Maybe I was exaggerating."

ME: "I think so. Good colleges accept students for a wide variety of reasons, like recommendations about them, their extracurricular activities, leadership abilities, and their community involvement. They want to graduate highly motivated people. It's not likely that one bad exam grade will keep you out of a good college as long as the rest of your high school career is solid."

TEEN: "I still think I might not get in."

ME: "Because of that one grade. Probably not."

TEEN: "Would you stop that!"

ME: "Only when you admit you're taking this one bad grade
  thing too far."
TEEN: "I took it too far."
ME: "What's a more realistic way to think?"
TEEN: "That if I do well overall I'll get to go to a good
  college."
ME: "What does it do to your mood when you think that way?"
TEEN: "It makes me feel better."
ME: "Good."

THE DOUBLE STANDARD

Children who are depressed have another way of thinking that is
hazardous to their emotional health. They often secretly employ a
double standard in which they judge themselves to be totally inad-
equate because they have a certain characteristic or make certain
mistakes. But they judge others who have the same characteristic
or make the same mistakes as being perfectly fine.

I recently had a conversation with a teenage girl who told me
that because she was overweight, she was essentially no good as a
human being. I asked her how overweight she judged herself to
be, and she stated that she was about thirty-five pounds overweight. I then asked her, out of curiosity, if in her eyes everyone
who was overweight by thirty-five pounds or more was no good as a
human being. She quickly said, "No." I asked her if I became
thirty-five pounds overweight, would I lose my worth as a human
being. She again said, "No." You can see how locked in her logic
she was. She judged only herself harshly and cut everyone else a
great amount of slack on the weight issue. She and I had some interesting talks about this. They went like this:

TEEN: "You're not going to make me talk about my weight
  again, are you?

M E : "No."

T E E N : "Good!"

M E : "We're going to talk some more about the way you think."

T E E N : "Oh no, not that again!"

M E : "Afraid so. I've got to figure out if you're still using that double standard. Are you still beating yourself up, saying bad things to yourself about yourself because of your weight, but judging anybody else who is overweight to be just fine?"

T E E N : "I probably am."

M E : "You haven't realized yet how bad it is to beat on yourself because of something like weight. You can change your weight, and you know that. The thing I really want you to see is that you beat yourself up about it, but you are nice to everyone else who is overweight."

T E E N : "I feel sorry for them. I know what they're going through. Somebody needs to be nice to them."

M E : "You also need to be nice to yourself."

T E E N : "I can't do that."

M E : "Let me ask you one of my weird questions."

T E E N : "Oh no, not another one of those."

M E : "Sorry. Would you be willing, next time you are thinking about your weight and really beating yourself up about it, to take yourself up to your bedroom, bend yourself over your bed and give yourself a good spanking?"

T E E N : "Are you out of your mind? That's the dumbest thing I ever heard of!"

M E : "I agree. Is it any dumber than you beating yourself up for being thirty-five pounds overweight, but being kind and forgiving toward your friends who are thirty-five pounds overweight?"

T E E N : "I get your point."

When you hear a double standard being used as part of a child's or adolescent's thinking, it is a clear hint that way down inside she is probably thinking lots of bad things about herself. While the issue of proof can become quite clouded and tricky, helping children and teenagers see their double standards can be relatively easy. The reason for this is that the double standard, once you point it out, is obviously an illogical way to think.

For example, if you are shy and think of yourself as a bad person because of your shyness, you can understand quite easily why it would be inappropriate to continue to think of me as a good person even though I was shy. A characteristic like shyness cannot mark one person as bad but leave the next person totally acceptable. Children and teenagers who employ double standards will admit this quite quickly when confronted about it. Yet often they continue to feel bad about themselves.

When you hear the double standard at work in your child's logic, do not forget to also probe deeper into how he feels about himself in general. You are likely to find that there are other hopeless beliefs rummaging around in his mind, each propped up by its own set of "proofs." You may need to attack each negative idea you encounter one by one.

THE FASCINATED EAR

The issues just discussed—structure, proof, and double standards—constitute the main underpinnings of depression. These are your targets. If you can successfully attack the problems with structure in your home, help your child avoid using illogical proofs in her thinking about herself, help her to reject using double standards when thinking about herself in comparison to others, help her to be resolute in not believing the things said to her by people who want her to feel bad about herself, and help her to commit to a plan to improve the aspects of her own behavior which truly do need improvement, then you will go a long way in helping her to defeat cognitive depression. You will find, though, that before you can talk about these issues, you have to make sure that you know how to listen.

You cannot help your child escape cognitive depression if you are unable or unwilling to listen with great interest and intensity. Children and adolescents can sense when someone is interested in them. The essential attributes of the fascinated ear are an interest in how the child or adolescent you are talking to sees and thinks about the world, an interest in what she is going through at present, and a desire to listen to her descriptions of the problems she is facing and the potential solutions she is thinking about.

Listening to your child in any meaningful way requires first and foremost that you spend time with her alone. By spending time alone, I do not mean talking with her while you are watching television or working around the house. Talking during these times is good, and not to be discounted, but it is not enough. You have to set aside blocks of time in which you and your child are going to do something that you both will enjoy. However, it must be something that cannot prevent you from interacting face to face.

Taking time to be alone with your child imparts the message that she is important and at the center of your concerns. If you have two children, as I do, it means finding the time to go out with each of them alone. In fact, it requires that both parents find time to spend with each child alone. If you have three children, time alone with each child makes your life more complicated from one viewpoint, I suppose, but even richer from another viewpoint.

A practical caution regarding going out alone with your child is that, ideally, you develop this habit prior to his reaching puberty. If he does not have you on his short list of "OK adults to be around" by the time he goes into adolescence, you are unlikely to make the list. If you have a history of doing things with him that are enjoyable, and he associates being around you as pleasant, he is much more likely to want to continue to spend time alone with you in his teenage years. Parents with the fascinated ear have a deep interest in who their children are becoming, how they think, what their values are, their taste in music and movies and friends, their career goals, and so on. And they take the time to communicate this fascination.

Your Ears Cannot Be Fully Open Until Your Mouth Is Fully Shut

You cannot develop the fascinated ear unless you are willing to keep your own mouth shut. Years ago during the early part of my training, I was required to sit with my clinical supervisor and go over the audio tapes of my sessions with clients at the training clinic in the Department of Counselor Education and Counseling Psychology at Western Michigan University. I remember playing one tape for him in which I was making what I thought were thoughtful, helpful suggestions. After listening for a few minutes, my supervisor, Dr. William Carlson, turned off the tape and said, "Don't just do something, sit there."

Just sitting there and listening, limiting your comments to brief questions and probes to help you find out more about what a child is thinking and feeling, is the hardest skill to learn when you are attempting to help. It is the most important skill, however, because the willingness to keep your comments and questions to a minimum is what often allows a child to talk and arrive at his own solution. Without realizing it, most of us put tremendous pressure on ourselves to come up with solutions for every imaginable problem children might present to us. While it feels nice to be the source of solutions, giving solutions too quickly prevents children from working through the process of discovering their own solutions. This philosophy is very much like the old saying about giving a hungry person a fish to eat, as opposed to teaching him how to fish.

When it comes to listening to children, parents seem to make mistakes along two lines. Often, they listen only briefly to what the

child is saying and then jump in and attempt to rescue him by of-
fering solutions and trying to solve his problems for him. Or they
listen only briefly to what the child is saying and jump in and attempt to prove him wrong about the negative things he is feeling
or thinking in hopes that doing so will somehow make him feel
better. An example of the first type of mistake might go like this:

> CHILD (sadly): "I got a D on my math test. I feel really stupid
> lately."
> PARENT: "You probably need to study more. I'm sure that
> would help."

An example of the second type of mistake would be:

> CHILD (again, sadly): "Nobody likes me. Jimmy is having a
> birthday party and I wasn't invited."
> PARENT: "Don't be silly. Everybody likes you."

While these kinds of strategies on the part of the parent are well
meant, in both cases the parent is failing to limit his comments to
brief questions or probes which will allow him to learn more about
the situation. Remember, if you can keep your child talking, there
is a good chance that his own talking will lead him to some solutions about what he is feeling and thinking. Your job, to reduce it
to the simplest terms, is to become a pleasant, caring person who
makes the child feel safe enough to open up and explore interior
thoughts and feelings. To return to the second example, it might
go better if done this way:

> CHILD: "Nobody likes me. Jimmy is having a birthday party,
> and I wasn't invited."
> PARENT: "Let's talk about it."
> CHILD: "Everybody else is going, but I didn't get invited."

PARENT: "When you say 'everybody,' do you mean the whole class?"

CHILD: "Well, most of the class."

PARENT: "Including your friends?"

CHILD: "Not all of them. Most of my friends don't usually hang out with Jimmy and his friends."

PARENT: "Who does Jimmy hang out with?"

CHILD: "Jimmy hangs out with Bobby and Jamal and Richard and those guys."

PARENT: "Do you hang out with those guys?"

CHILD: "Not really."

PARENT: "Help me understand why you're upset about not getting invited."

CHILD: "I just don't like being left out. It seems like everybody else is popular but me."

In this example, you can see that while it took some doing, the parent helped his son get down to the core issue, the issue of not feeling popular enough. This is the way it often works when talking to depressed children and adolescents. They begin with one thing, but if you keep them talking, they eventually wind their way on down into the real things that are bothering them. All roads lead to Rome, as they say.

In the example above, once the parent realizes that the child is thinking he is not popular enough, the parent can begin to search for proof that this is indeed true. For example, does he get phone calls from his peers asking him to play? When he invites others over, do they readily come or do they make excuses to avoid him? If it turns out that the child is being socially rejected by his peers, then the parent's job becomes one of trying to find out how to enhance his son's social skills so that he is increasingly included in social events. If it turns out, however, that he tends to get invited about as much as everyone else, has about as many friends as everyone else, and is generally as accepted by his peers as everyone else, then the parent's job becomes one of helping his son to understand that his negative thoughts about his own social acceptance, which are making him feel sad and dejected, are not grounded in reality to begin with. It is likely that once his parents help him realize that he is being far too hard on himself and is thinking things about himself that are not grounded in reality, he will begin to feel better.

Suspending Your Own Viewpoint

There are several other attributes to the fascinated ear. Listening with the fascinated ear requires that you be willing to suspend your own viewpoint long enough to learn about your child's viewpoint. You are guaranteed to never learn anything about your children if you just assume they think like you.

There is nothing implied in suspending your own viewpoint that says you must agree with what your child says. If you don't take the time to listen fully and show your child that you are interested in her opinions, she will sense that you don't really care about what she thinks. Once she comes to that opinion, she probably won't give you the chance to engage her in the type of talk that can help correct her mistaken beliefs.

Listening with a fascinated ear also requires that you not take your child's depressed mood and behavior personally. Children and teenagers often express depression through cranky, aggressive behavior. Depressed children and teens can be explosive and out of control because they are so frustrated with the way they see their lives going. If you get swept up into their mood, you yourself can begin to yell, scream, and shout. While your yelling might make your depressed child become quiet, she becomes so only out of fear. By yelling, you have shown her that now no one is in control. This outcome cannot possibly make her feel safer. And it cannot make you feel better either. You must have enough ego boundary, as it is called, to not allow your child's frustration to bleed over into you, causing you to act like her.

Another attribute of the fascinated ear is communicating to your child that she is free to tell you anything about how she is feeling and thinking without you going into full-blown panic. You will be rightfully frightened if your daughter tells you that she wants to kill herself. But if you *show* that you are overly frightened, it may make her even more frightened about what she is going through and convince her that no one can handle the problems she is facing. Once this happens she is likely to clam up, thinking that what she is going through is so bad that it should not be talked about. Children and teenagers need their parents to remain calm in the face of bad news, because doing so makes the children feel safe.

Encountering "I don't know"

To get inside the mind of the depressed child often only takes being alone with him and saying to him, "Tell me how you've been feeling about yourself lately." After you ask this, be prepared to listen for various themes to emerge. In particular, listen for evidence that one or more of the ten hopeless beliefs is alive and well inside your child's thinking process.

Of course, not every child or teenager will open up. In the field of psychology this is known as resistance, the conscious or unconscious unwillingness to allow you in. While some children will give you a veritable flood of information about how they have been feeling and thinking once you ask them, others will reply to your questions about their thoughts and feelings only by saying, "I don't know."

You want to be open to the idea that for many children "I don't know" is a truthful answer. Many children who are depressed due to how they are thinking or due to external stressors will be able to tell you something about their thoughts and feelings and recent experiences. Many will not. In situations like this, you need to be able to take the ten hopeless beliefs and turn them into probes that can help you test and examine your child's thoughts. A tip on how to do this is to ask your child if she has been having "secret thoughts about . . ." Doing so gives the child permission to go ahead and speak what has until now remained unspoken. An example of probing for negative ideas might go like this:

PARENT: "I'm curious about how you've been feeling lately."
CHILD: "I don't know."
PARENT (considering Hopeless Belief #1: I am made of inferior stuff): "I was wondering how you've been feeling about yourself lately. You know, if you've been having secret thoughts about not being good enough, and stuff like that."
CHILD: "I sure don't feel like I'm good enough."
PARENT: "Why's that?"
CHILD: "Because everybody else does everything better than me."

You can see now that the child has opened up the idea that she is not feeling like she fares well in comparison to her peers. The parent's job, once this idea is opened up, is to help her find out if her thoughts are based in reality or not. Again, if her thoughts have a real basis, the parent's next step is to help her child more clearly define her areas of weakness and help her to make realistic plans to improve. If her thoughts turn out not to be grounded in reality, the parent must then help her to see that she is making herself feel bad by thinking negative things that have no basis in truth.

If using these types of probes, which get at your child's private thoughts about herself, are not productive, your next strategy is to use probes that get at external stressors. Does she feel overwhelmed by too much homework, or is someone in the neighborhood or school picking on her, or is there something going on at home that is bothering her? These are straightforward questions that can potentially give you clear information on what needs to be done.

If you have asked questions about your child's internal thoughts and external stressors and you are still coming up dry in terms of why she seems depressed, there are two further possibilities to consider. Children who are acting depressed, but who genuinely cannot tell you anything about why they feel the way they feel, may be suffering from a biochemical-based depression. Given that such depressions can be traced back to chemical reactions in the brain, it is unlikely that children can shed any light on why they feel the way they do. Also, it is possible that your child is suffering from anxiety, rather than depression, as one of the hallmarks of anxious children is an inability to tell you why they feel the way they feel.

When you are certain that something is bothering your child or teenager and your offers to talk are met with strong resistance, you need to remain quietly persistent. Instead of using probes and questions, begin to make clear declarative statements to your child about his behavior and about your concerns. When encountering strong resistance, you need to let your child know that not talking is not an option, because you are aware that he is feeling bad and things are at a point where something must be done. Be careful to remain calm in such situations. You may run into situations in which your child or teenager is protecting his depression because he doesn't want anyone to know his private thoughts or feelings. He perceives your probes and questions as an invasion.

Children and teens who use "I don't know" as an excuse and whose strategies revolve around not disclosing their inner thoughts will often move rapidly toward an explosion in an attempt to back you off. If you explode in return or if you take their explosion personally, you will fall right into the trap. If you do explode, make sure that you hit your own reset button as quickly as possible and prepare yourself to make another attempt to talk after the situation has calmed down. Do not simply give up because your child or teenager finds it unpleasant to talk. Walking away in the face of knowing that something bad is going on inside of your child, even when he is insisting that you leave him alone, acts only to keep his depressed state intact. Again, the main points to remember in such situations are: First, you are the parent and, as such, are in charge in your household. Second, unknown to your child, you will be willing to repeat yourself over and over in order to make it clear that not talking is not an option. For example:

PARENT: "The past few weeks you've seemed more sad and angry than I've ever seen you before. I'd like to help."

TEEN: "I told you I don't want to talk."

PARENT: "I understand that you don't want to talk. But you need to understand that as your parent my job is to make sure that everything is going well in your life. That's why we need to talk."

TEEN: "I told you to leave me alone. Just get out of my face and leave me alone!"

PARENT: "Leaving you alone is not one of the options. Like I just said, I'm the parent and my job is to find out what is going on in your life that is making you act so sad and angry."

TEEN: "If you don't shut up I'm going out the door!"

PARENT: "That would be a bad decision on your part and would just make this more complicated. I would hate to have to punish you while you're feeling so bad about something else, but if you continue to act in such a disrespectful manner, I will. I will tell you again, as your parent I need to know why you have been feeling so sad and angry lately."

TEEN: "I told you, it's none of your damn business!"

PARENT: "I'm going to warn you again about being
disrespectful to me when I'm trying to help you."

TEEN: "I already told you I don't want your help."

PARENT: "And as I already told you, not talking is not an
option. You need to begin to tell me what is going on with
you lately. If you won't do it now, we will have this
conversation again soon. I'm worried about you, and not
talking in situations like this will never be an option in this
household."

This is obviously a difficult situation. You can see that the parent
has claimed her "parental role" quite successfully, in that she is
not getting baited into an argument and is making it quite clear
that she is the parent and her child is the child and that those two
roles will not be changed in the power structure of the family. In
general, some children and teens will fight tooth and nail not to
talk and then, finally relenting, feel quite relieved to have talked.

REPLACEMENT BELIEFS

When your discussions go well, your child or teenager will talk to
you about her mood and inner beliefs and will be able to understand that her negative beliefs are causing her to be depressed. She
may even show good insight into the idea that she needs to get rid
of her hopeless beliefs about herself and replace them with more
positive and realistic ways of thinking. Still, she may not be able to
figure out a whole new set of beliefs. This is when you have to be
willing to help her develop what I refer to as replacement beliefs.
Replacement beliefs are new beliefs which are less negative and
more grounded in reality.

Do I believe that it is actually reasonable for a parent to tell her
child how he should think? The answer is yes, of course. I've often

described the minds of children and teenagers as chaos factories and faulty devices. While your child or teen may be quite bright, he does not have the life experience to know which of his beliefs are reasonable and which are, to use a highly scientific, clinical term, just plain goofy.

• • •

In the chapters that follow, we will go into replacement beliefs for each of the hopeless beliefs that cause depression. In general, instead of continuing to harbor the ten hopeless beliefs listed in the introduction, you want your child or teenager to realize the following:

- Negative thinking causes depression.
- It is possible for my own thoughts to fool me into thinking something about myself that is not true. This can lead me into feeling depressed for no real reason.
- None of my weaknesses or faults are so large that they can't be fixed.
- I need real proof. I will fix what I do wrong or poorly. I will not worry about the bad things that people say about me that are not true.

We are now ready to go into the ten hopeless beliefs in greater detail. As you read each of the case studies, ask yourself what techniques you might use if the children or teenagers we are talking about were yours. As we examine the cases, we will be looking at structure, proof, or use of double standards to see how cognitive depression got its start and how it has been maintained. The ultimate goal is to learn how it can be defeated.

Chapter 2

Death Is an Option

Not every child or adolescent who is depressed will have suicidal thoughts. Many do, however, and it is important that before you spend too much time thinking about the other nine Hopeless Beliefs that cause depression in children and adolescents, you make sure that Hopeless Belief #1 is not dominating your child's thinking.

When a child or adolescent tells me that he wants to die, I do not move too quickly into trying to talk him out of it. While it is understandable that any parent will feel the urge to make these thoughts go away as quickly as possible, to do so would be too much like trying to change the subject when someone tells you they have something really important to talk to you about. If you want to help to prevent your child's death, it is best to first understand why he wants to die. That requires allowing him to talk.

Thoughts of death get formed when a child or adolescent comes to believe that he has no way out of what he is feeling or experiencing. Children and teenagers kill themselves because they don't believe that the way they feel will ever change. It goes without saying that they believe they can no longer tolerate how they feel. They kill themselves out of a belief that they are not worthy enough as human beings to remain alive. Or they kill themselves to get revenge on someone, such as a boyfriend or girlfriend who has broken up with them, or a parent who they think is too critical, or schoolmates who rejected them.

When I talk to a child or teenager about the idea of dying, one of the first things I want to know is what he means by the words *die* and *dead*. These words are certainly open to interpretation. For some children they may mean entering eternal oblivion. For others they mean entering eternal life. Many children and teenagers have the notion that they can be dead yet still be around others as invisible beings, able to watch what their friends and family are doing without being seen. One boy told me that he wanted to see who would come to his funeral. He had the impression that he would be hovering in the air, ten feet or so over the crowd. Then he would know who really cared about him and who didn't. Many children and adolescents believe that it would be fun to be able to do the things that ghosts do.

Children and teenagers also seem to believe that death can improve the way they feel. They tell me that they will feel better once they are dead or that once they are dead they won't have to feel the way they feel now, as if there will be some new way of feeling after they die.

Also, it is important to find out how serious a child is when he says he wants to die. Many children say it out of frustration, not really wanting to die. Many say it because they know that it is guaranteed to get a parent's attention.

INTERPRETING THOUGHTS OF DEATH

The process of questioning and talking is what helps parents and therapists understand whether or not a child is truly serious about the idea of dying. Once I am convinced that a child or teenager really means what he is saying, I ask him to try to view his thoughts of death in a new way. I ask him if, once he thinks about it, he really wants his physical existence to cease. Or is it possible that what he really wants is for the way he is feeling to die?

Most people give a sigh of relief at this suggestion, and they tend to find this alternative interpretation of the death thought to be comforting. Prior to finding a new way to interpret these thoughts, many children and teenagers have the belief that because they are thinking of death, they *have to* die.

Why Joe Wanted to Die

Coming to believe that death is an option is a complex process. Typically, children and teenagers arrive at that conclusion after having passed through several of the other beliefs on our list. It is also certainly possible to arrive at that point due to external stressors or due to biochemical imbalances. All three should be explored when death is the issue.

Let me tell you the story about Joe. His mother called my office in a total panic one morning, having gotten my name from Joe's pediatrician. Joe's girlfriend had told him that morning at school that she intended to break up with him. This sent Joe, who was fifteen, into a dizzying tailspin. He had been going with her for about ten months. Like too many people his age, he had made her the center of his life. He believed that they would be together all through high school and eventually get married. Joe had been taken to the principal's office because he was telling friends in the hallway that he wanted to die and that he was going to kill himself.

The reason that I will never forget Joe has nothing to do with his particular situation. It has to do with the way he entered my office. He was propped up on both sides—on one side by his mother and on the other side by the girl who had broken up with him just hours earlier. Joe had his arms around each woman's neck and shoulders. They walked him down the hallway in the way that two soldiers might walk a compatriot whose legs no longer work. They walked him into my office and placed him on my couch.

The girlfriend stayed only long enough to introduce herself. Helping him get to the psychologist's office was her last official act of the relationship, she said, and she made it clear that once he was safe, she was "outta here."

Joe's face was swollen and puffy with tears, and he could hardly talk. He spent the first few minutes in my office just crying on his mother's shoulder. His mother provided some family history while he sat and tried to collect himself.

Joe lived with his mother and his younger sister. His parents were divorced, and Joe rarely saw his father. He was an indifferent student. While bright and, according to his teachers, capable of getting A's and B's, he did only enough work to get by. As he explained after I got to know him, he would work hard the last two weeks of each marking period to bring his F's up to C's.

He spent his spare time watching television when his girlfriend wasn't available. Otherwise, he was at her house, or she was at his house, or they were on the phone with each other. He had no male friends or associates and no social life outside of what he did with his girlfriend, her family, or his own mother and sister. He had no interests in traditional "guy" activities, such as sports, cars, or outdoor activities, and he did little with his girlfriend other than make out. They had been sexually active for a number of months, although his mother did not seem to be aware of this.

Joe's mother indicated that she had no control of him, but she was quick to add that he was not a bad young man at all. He did not run the streets, did not skip school, and was generally pleasant to be around. As I got to know him, I also learned that he had a desire to study electronics after high school, but he wanted to go to the easiest program possible because he didn't like to work hard. He struck me as being almost totally unburdened by ambition.

One of my first probes with Joe was to find out if he truly

intended to kill himself. He answered that he did. I wanted to know if he had chosen a time, place, and a method to kill himself, and he said that he had. He told me that he had heard that taking a large dose of a certain over-the-counter medication could put him into a coma and shut down his liver. He also stated that he had considered slitting his wrists, but in a way that would be much more lethal than the method that lots of teenagers attempt.

• • •

If your child tells you that he wants to kill himself, you need to ask these very same questions. While any threat of suicide should be treated with great seriousness, threats that contain a credible method for killing one's self should obviously not be ignored. In general, males choose more violent methods than females. The point would be, however, that if your child tells you he has a method that will work, you want to treat it like the emergency it is.

• • •

I asked Joe to tell me about why he wanted to die. He replied that dying was a way for him to escape the pain that he was feeling. This led us into a discussion about how to interpret his desire to die. I asked Joe if he truly wanted his physical existence to cease forever or if it were possible that he just wanted the way he was feeling to die.

There are philosophical reasons behind this question. While I am far from being a scholar in comparative religion, it is my understanding that most of the world's religions have in common the cycle of birth, death, and rebirth. In my experience it has been quite rare to encounter someone who pointedly wanted to just die, to just simply cease existing, with no interest at all in being reborn into a less painful life.

Joe liked the interpretation that I put on his death-oriented thinking. He said that he would indeed like to no longer feel what he was feeling at the moment and that the idea of entering eternal oblivion did not appeal to him once he thought about it. He liked the idea of working with me, the goal being to have the way he was feeling die while he remained physically among the living.

This was not a breakthrough point, however. Joe was highly emotional. Later, as I got to know him, I came to understand that he could be dramatically indecisive. During our early sessions, he would go from hopeful and philosophical one moment to weepy and telling me that life without his girlfriend was truly not worth living the next moment.

This meant that we had to go further into another "hopeless belief." The main idea gripping Joe's thinking was "Death is an option." As is usual, "Death is an option" was the fire that was being fueled by something else, in this case by "I can't live without this person." This is the way it tends to go when the death thought rears its ugly head. Death is the solution to problems that are being caused by a second, and sometimes a third, issue. It is rare that it pops up all by itself.

It was clear that Joe's emotions were bouncing all about. In order to stabilize him, it was important to help him see that his belief that death remained an option was a mistaken belief that could, at worst, cost him his life and toss his entire family into chaos. I had to force him further into the question of whether or not death was truly an option he wanted to exercise. I do this with children and teenagers by appealing to their interests in the material world and in the future.

I began to ask him questions like: Are you sure you've done everything you ever wanted to do? Are there any places you'd like to see before you die? Are there any movies you'd like to see? Are there any cars you'd like to own before you die? Wouldn't you like the chance to live on your own, with your own apartment, and buy a monster stereo?

I used a term with Joe that I often employ in my work. I told him that what he was going through was "painfully normal." By that, I meant that there was no such thing as a painless breakup and that he was having an experience that every teenager is guaranteed to have. I encourage parents to use this phrase with their children and adolescents not only when they experience the loss of a relationship, as in Joe's case, but when they encounter other personal disappointments or failures. I told Joe that he had to learn to think of the breakup of his relationship as being the emotional equivalent of stepping on a nail—bound to hurt like hell for quite a while, but also guaranteed to get better if given time to heal.

Joe and I also talked about the nature of death. I reported to him that if it was a state that he was bent upon entering, I at least wanted to know what he thought it would be like. Like a lot of teenagers, he had the belief that he would "feel better" once he was dead. I told him that as far as I know scientifically, he wouldn't be feeling anything. No pain, for sure, but also no pleasure. Nothing. Nada.

Joe didn't like that idea. He thought, somehow, that after he was dead he could still see people and be aware of what they were saying or doing. He told me that he wanted to see the look on his girlfriend's face when she learned that he was dead. I asked him how he could go about pulling off that particular feat.

I think the lights came on for Joe when he heard himself say out loud that he wanted to see the look on his girlfriend's face when she learned that he was dead. It happens this way often in counseling and psychotherapy. Someone may think something privately and develop a strong belief in it. However, once they speak it out loud, they realize that the idea is riddled with holes.

Structure in Joe's Life

If we analyze Joe's story, we find a number of issues that deserve consideration. We'll return to the issue of structure. In Joe's case, the home structure he was living in was too porous. From my viewpoint, there were not enough clear standards, expectations, and limits. Joe could stay out pretty much as late as he wanted to, although I should reiterate that he was not one to abuse this privilege. Joe could also pretty much live as he wanted to in his own home. He did not like it when I told his mother that it was not a good idea for him to entertain his girlfriend in his bedroom, behind closed doors. Also, I told Joe's mother that there was nothing wrong with demanding better grades from him, given that he was capable. I asked her to consider connecting his driving privileges to his academic performance. He did not like this, but he understood it.

Joe also suffered from lack of contact with an adult male mentor. He had no idea about how to go about forming a relationship with a girl because no one had ever given him any guidelines. He took his cues from his lovesick male peers, from movies, and from television. Because of this he was totally confused about boundaries and limits. He did not know how to say "No" to his girlfriend and could not tolerate it when she said it to him.

One of my first talks with Joe's mother involved telling her that he needed a considerable amount of coaching about what was appropriate in a teenage relationship and what was not. I told her that he needed consistent contact with appropriate male relatives and peers or needed to make contact with someone who could informally serve as a big brother. More than anything, however, I worked to convince her that the rules and standards had to come from her, not from him.

The Issue of Proof in Joe's Life

Joe also needed to encounter the idea that he had no real proof that suicide was a reasonable way of dealing with the pain of his loss. When you read how therapists question someone about killing himself, it might sound as if the questions were brutal. In actuality, they are asked in calm, clear, and caring tones. You should also keep in mind that asking pointed questions about death and dying does not bother the suicidal individual. In order to reach the conclusion that death is an option, they have asked themselves horrible questions many times over. I believe that they actually want someone else to ask them the questions they have already pondered because, secretly, they hope to come to some other conclusion which will let them reject oblivion. It is important to talk to them about all of the following points.

First of all, suicidal individuals will tell you that they are not afraid of death. You have to try to let them know that the eerie calmness they feel in the face of death is not a natural state of mind but is, rather, proof that they are exceptionally depressed. Depression can leave people so depleted that they have little emotion at all, including no appropriate fear of the vast terror they should be experiencing while staring death in the face.

I asked Joe to continue to resist the urge to kill himself until his feelings came back and he didn't feel so emotionally blunted from his loss. I told him that it was very important to never make a large decision while depressed, because invariably he would regret it. I remember that he challenged me on this. He said, "You want me to wait until I feel good to think about killing myself, when you know that once I feel good, I won't want to kill myself."

"Precisely," I responded.

Second, it is important to talk to suicidal children and teenagers about the experiences of other people who have made suicide attempts which brought them right up to the brink of death but failed to push them over the edge. I tell them that the people I have known who survived their suicide attempt without serious damage are happy that they survived. Each one of them, at the point of thinking that they were about to slip away, began to panic and realized clearly that they did not want to die. While we will never know the thoughts of the dying person who did slip beyond life's grasp, the ones who were pulled back from the brink are often thankful for having gotten a second chance.

Children and teenagers also have the notion that taking an overdose of pills will allow them to slip away quietly, without pain. They need to understand that suicide survivors have told me that this is quite often not the case. The body does not respond well to toxic amounts of medication, and the dying process can be exceptionally painful as the liver begins to shut down. It is probably good to tell suicidal teenagers that many people who overdose on medication actually end up dying because they begin to convulse at some point and drown in their own vomit. Children and teenagers don't like details like this. Joe didn't, and I suspect that it helped stop his suicidal thinking.

I also tell suicidal children and teenagers about the few people I have met who made highly lethal suicide attempts which they survived, but which left them damaged for life. The survivor I most often tell them about is the man who tried to blow his brains out. His hand was shaking so much that the gun slipped and he shot himself in the head at an angle such that the bullet skimmed across his brain, leaving him partially paralyzed and barely able to talk. He told me that at the moment he pulled the trigger he panicked, and he knew in that split second that he did not want to die.

This man's condition also leads me into talking to them about the impact that a severe injury, or actual death, has on family and relatives. Many people who attempt suicide do so because they are angry and want to make others feel bad for not having treated them better. This is almost always unsuccessful, because the surviving family members end up being angry at the suicider for killing himself, thinking of him as selfish, self-centered, weak, and unwilling or unable to think about the impact of his behavior on others. I have never met a surviving family member who thought of the suicider as a noble martyr.

Regardless of the suicidal individual's motive, family members and friends invariably will come to think of the suicider as being mentally ill. Suicidal teenagers, in particular, do not like the idea that they will come to be thought of as mentally ill. This is another one of the details that can sometimes help make them reconsider.

A third approach for children and teenagers who are religious is to attempt to influence them with theological perspectives on suicide. Many of the teenagers I have worked with have told me that they cannot get into heaven if they kill themselves, and a few have told me that they would go to hell. The notion is that it is a sin to destroy God's creation. I see nothing wrong with using such theological positions if it will save a life.

And as a fourth way to try to get Joe to reject his suicidal thoughts, I talked to him using some word tricks designed to help move him past his sense of hopelessness. I would say things to him like, "You're telling me that your life cannot *possibly* be any good at all if you don't marry your girlfriend?" He would say yes. I would then reply, "I don't understand how your life could not *possibly* be any good, ever, if you don't marry this girl. You're telling me that you cannot *possibly* ever have any real fun with anyone else?" The trick, of course, was to get Joe to admit that it was at least a possibility that he could eventually have some fun with other girls and grow attached to them. Once he admitted that it was a possibility, I never let him forget that he said it. The point of this was to help him understand that there was indeed hope for the future.

Joe's Double Standards

Sometimes Joe would be so trapped by his own logic that I would have to make him aware of his double standards. He hated this, because it illustrated to him so clearly how his own logic was what was keeping him unhappy. But pointing out his double standards to him also helped him regain his sense of hope.

I would say something like, "You will never be happy because you did not marry your first serious girlfriend." He would say yes. Then I would say, "So your life cannot possibly be happy because you did not marry your first serious girlfriend." He would agree again. I would then point out to him that he was using a double standard. If he could never be happy because he didn't marry his first serious girlfriend, how could anyone else who did not marry their first serious girlfriend ever be happy? Given that most high school relationships don't result in marriage, how could anybody ever end up being happy?

Joe would tell me that this was just true for him, not for everybody. I would then ask why it was that he had a set of rules that applied only to him and everyone else had another set of rules. He would get flustered with my argument, which was exactly the point I wanted him to arrive at. I wanted him to clearly see that his own logic was trapping him. If he could bring himself to at least entertain the possibility that it was reasonable to be hopeful about his future, he would eventually feel better.

• • •

Joe's story has a happy ending, at least in part. I saw him frequently at first, and then on a more sporadic basis. We worked together, all told, for about a year. He came to understand clearly that death was not an option that he wished to exercise because it was more preferable to remain among the living and take the good with the bad. He began to date other girls, and at some point in time the girl who had broken up with him put a great deal of pressure on him to get back together. He refused, telling her that he didn't want to get back into the kind of relationship that they had earlier been in. He came to believe that it was too intense and wasn't healthy. He told me that he didn't think the loss of any relationship was worth killing himself over. I never got him to exercise his true academic potential, though. He continued on his path of just doing enough work at the end of each grading period to get by, no doubt driving his teachers crazy.

THE BOY WHO WISHED HE NEVER WAS

We turn now to Freddy. His mother was worried sick when she called my office. She said that her son, age five and a half, didn't seem to enjoy playing with his friends or toys lately. His appetite had fallen off, and he was beginning to stay to himself too much. What bothered her most, though, were the things he said.

On meeting him, my first impression was that he was a little boy with an angelic face, but a face that was entirely too serious. He seemed like a five-year-old dressed in a gray, three-piece suit.

I asked Freddy and his mother to come back to my office. Once seated, he grew still and stared out the window. His mother said to him, "Tell Doctor Riley what you told me yesterday."

Freddy looked at me and said, "I told my mom I wish I never was."

I didn't want to assume too much, so I looked back at him and said, "You wish you never were what?"

He looked at me even more intently. "I just wish I never was."

Freddy, whom I rapidly began to realize was very bright, explained, "It's not that I want to die. And it's not that I want to kill myself. I just wish I had never existed to begin with. You couldn't die if you had never existed to begin with."

I remember the stillness in the room after he said this. He and his mother were still, I suppose, because Freddy had made himself perfectly clear and they were awaiting my response. I was still because I had never heard such a young child say something quite so profound. I finally asked back, "Why do you wish you had never existed?"

"Because of the way I feel inside," he said.

As he talked, I realized that he enjoyed nothing and looked forward to nothing. Worst of all, he had no sense of hope that things would get better. To make things even more complicated, there was nothing in Freddy's recent history that could account for how he was feeling. He was from a stable home, with an involved father and a very nurturing, loving mother. There had been no recent family illnesses, deaths, personal failures, unexpected large changes, or other possible triggers. His parents got along well, and Freddy got along well with everyone in his family. Kindergarten had been a breeze for him, and he had plenty of friends. He had always liked himself just fine. He didn't have any history of self-concept problems or, as I term it, believing any "hopeless beliefs." Freddy's life, from all that we could see, was built on a solid foundation.

At some level, thoughts and feelings can be seen as the tangible manifestation of the brain's biochemical workings. Given that we could find no psychological or environmental causes for Freddy's depression, I suggested to his mother that we have him evaluated further for medication.

Freddy was fortunate in that his pediatrician maintained a strong interest in depression and had specialized training in treating young children with antidepressants. I suggested to Freddy's mother that we also talk to him several times about how he was thinking and offer support to make sure that his sad thinking did not turn overtly suicidal. I also made some of the standard suggestions that I make to parents whose young children are depressed: Make sure he gets lots more lap time and physical affection. Make sure he gets taken out to do things that he has always found to be fun in the past. Be sure to praise him. Make sure he has plenty of contact with his friends. His mother diligently followed these suggestions, as best I could tell.

Freddy continued to say for the next few weeks that regardless of everything we were doing for him, he still wished that he had never been. Then one day, his mother told me that it seemed like she had her little boy back again. Clearly, it seemed that the antidepressant medication had begun to take effect. His mood rapidly became less somber, and he began to seem more boylike again.

Freddy's story is another one with a happy ending. Once he seemed stable, we discontinued counseling, with the provision that his mother would check in with me by phone from time to time. She was to update me on his progress or let me know if she was seeing indications of danger. About six months after Freddy began to feel better, his pediatrician decided to slowly discontinue the medication. It has been a while since I have heard from his mother, but at last report, he continued to be a happy little boy.

EXTERNAL STRESS AND DEATH THOUGHTS: THE SOLs

Virginia, where I live, is at the forefront of the growing national craze to use a set of standardized tests to determine if children can move on to the next grade level. These tests are called the Standards of Learning, popularly known as the SOLs. When first conceptualized, the idea was that you could not move forward unless you passed the test. This was regardless of how well you might have done otherwise in school. You could be an honor roll student, but if you were not good at taking standardized tests and failed the SOLs, you would be retained to get all A's on the same material again next year. Thankfully, the public is beginning to raise dire concerns about using standardized tests in such a draconian form, and the State Board of Education seems to be listening.

When I was a child, the term "SOL" referred to a phrase that cannot be mentioned here. Suffice it to say that if you were SOL, you were seriously out of luck, so to speak. In Virginia, the SOLs have left many children feeling SOL, to the extent that this spring, when the tests were administered across several grade levels, we had a flood of parents of worried, stressed-out children calling my office for appointments. Among them was one preadolescent boy who had told his mother that if he did not pass his SOLs, he intended to kill himself.

Granted, this is not the typical reaction that you would expect from a child who is having difficulty with a test. Had his been an isolated case, I would have placed the locus of his difficulties more within his self-concept or would have been much more prone to think that he was an overly anxious child or a perfectionistic child who did not know how to deal with academic pressure. However, there were many, many other parents calling who indicated that these tests were stressing their children out.

The major stressor for this young man was external to his thinking and his biological functioning. His case illustrates that external stressors can make a child or teenager just as depressed as biochemical imbalances and hopeless beliefs. The first thing we talked to him about was the fact that his parents simply would not allow him to be held back on the basis of one standardized test taken only one time.

These were the other points we talked about: His grades were fine. He was known to be serious and hard working. None of his teachers had ever talked to his parents about him needing to be retained. His own teacher had told him not to worry, because at this point the tests were still considered experimental, and no one could be retained on the basis of SOL scores alone for a couple of years to come. His teachers also told him that it would be very unlikely that schools would adopt a policy of retaining children who otherwise were doing well in school. Given all of this, we convinced him that he had nothing to worry about and that there was no need for him to think of death as an option.

WHAT TO DO IF YOUR CHILD IS SUICIDAL

In overview, should you ever find that your child or adolescent is experiencing suicidal ideation, your first response should be to remain calm, and your second response should be to get her to talk about her thoughts and feelings. It is imperative to immediately seek the help of a mental health professional who has experience in working with suicidal children and teenagers. Your child's pediatrician or family doctor is the best source of information on mental health providers in your area.

It is unlikely, however, that counseling and medications alone will be sufficient interventions. As the parent, you need to do your own analysis of the structure in your home, such as arguing, fighting, substance use, or emotionally unavailable parents, and go about resolving any problems that you find. You need to try to pinpoint external sources of stress that might be dragging your child down, such as school pressures, peer rejection, or personal failures, and do whatever is necessary to relieve the stress. You need to consider the idea of medication, because in combination with counseling it is the most effective way to help your child get past a difficult period of time.

You'll want to engage in lots of talk with your child or teen, so that you can find out exactly what her ideas are and what proofs she is using to support those ideas. You need to be ready to help her see which of her ideas are not grounded in reality and help her to develop a more reasonable set of beliefs about herself so that she does not face the unnecessary pressures of dealing with problems that do not exist to begin with. If she has to face negative things about herself that are grounded in reality, you have to help her develop a plan for changing those things. Mainly, you have to keep her focused on the idea that the future can bring change and that she is likely to feel much better with time and effort.

You want to help the suicidal child or adolescent take an exceptionally hard look at the thinking behind the desire to die. This thinking is faulty, obviously, as healthy individuals are driven toward life and accomplishment instead of toward death. Here are examples of the replacement beliefs a child must learn in order to overcome suicidal depression:

- Suicidal thoughts never mean that you *have* to die. They are just indicators of how truly bad you feel.
- It is doubtful that you really want your physical existence to cease. It is much more likely that you want the way you are feeling to die.
- People only want to kill themselves when they are deeply depressed. You should never make any important decision when you are deeply depressed.
- No failed relationship is worth dying over. The hurt you feel after losing a boyfriend or a girlfriend is normal pain. It will go away with time.
- Everyone experiences trouble with school and peers, sooner or later. This kind of trouble also comes under the heading of "painfully normal," and not worth dying over.

Fortunately, most depressed children and teenagers are not suicidal. This is not to imply that cognitive depression absent suicidal ideation is a pleasant state of mind. As we shall continue to see, there are a host of thoughts that have the power to make our children perfectly miserable. Fortunately, we can help them get through each one.

Chapter 3

I Am Made of Inferior Stuff

A number of years ago I worked with a high school senior who came to see me suffering from a state of depression that appeared to be powered by a desperate level of self-hatred. Laura's case provides an excellent example of what happens to children and teens who secretly harbor the belief that they are not good enough. As I got to know her, I quickly became aware of three things she believed about herself with all seriousness: She believed that she was ugly; she believed that she was stupid; she believed that no desirable boy would ever ask her out. All of this combined to give her the feeling that she was made of inferior stuff.

The particulars of her case are interesting. On hearing that she believed herself to be ugly, stupid, and undesirable, you might be forming the mental picture of an unattractive girl with questionable intellectual abilities and no social skills. This could not be further from the truth. She was strikingly tall, with waist-length hair. I privately thought that her eye makeup was a bit overdone and that her blue jeans seemed profoundly tight, almost painted on (the style of the day, compared to the potato sacks that pass for blue jeans as I write today). It was clear, regardless of what she thought about her own appearance, that it would not be possible for her to walk through the mall without the heads of most teenage males swiveling hypnotically in her direction.

The Six Foot Girl, as I came to call Laura, had been raised in a family of tall, cold, emotionally distant people. Her father taught her through his behavior and attitude to believe that women have little intrinsic worth and that their best option is to keep themselves looking good enough to attract a man with money.

While she was forthcoming about the ideas of feeling dumb, it took quite a while for her to trust me enough to finally confide that she felt ugly. She believed that the shape of her nose, which was small and pixylike, not long, thin, and aquiline, was the fatal flaw that would prevent a desirable young man from finding her attractive. She had come to the conclusion that the only males who would want her were the losers, and she had taken up with a nasty-tempered boyfriend who was hitting her.

After I was certain that she trusted me and that she had a good sense of humor, I decided to use the idea of "proof" in an attempt to help explode the negative things she was thinking about herself. I told her that I was going to say something that would no doubt strike her as unexpected for a psychologist to say. I promised her that ultimately it would make her laugh and would not be harmful, but that she would find it to be surprising at first. "I am a reasonable man," I told her. "If you say you are ugly, stupid, and undesirable, I am willing to believe you." I startled her, until I added the last part of my sentence. "I am willing to believe you. *All you have to do is give me real proof.*"

She wanted to know what I meant by "proof." I told her that it was the nature of depression to warp perception and reality, to make perfectly good people dislike themselves for no real reason, while out in the real world perfectly bad people were running around feeling just fine about themselves. I told her that as long as she was going to think such bad things about herself, she had to have real evidence that they were true. Otherwise, she would have to admit that she was willing to believe just about anything, regardless of whether or not it could be shown to be true.

I asked her to begin by telling me more about the idea that she was stupid. I let her know that simply because she believed herself to be stupid did not constitute proof that she was stupid.

She said that she had never thought about the idea of proof. She had just always *felt* stupid. This is usually the case with individuals who suffer from self-hatred. They rarely stop to question their negative beliefs which make them feel depressed but have no grounding in reality.

People mired in self-hatred are usually hesitant to take a really close look at their beliefs. There are reasons for this. Beliefs such as "I'm stupid" or "I'm ugly" are so hot, so radioactive, that the person suffering from them rarely wants to pick them up and examine them. It hurts too much to do so. Or maybe it is too scary to take such a close look at yourself. In Laura's case, the negative beliefs, the hopeless beliefs, were foisted on her by her hypercritical father, the weight of whose authority seemed so vast to her that she dared not challenge him. It became easier just to accept what he said, never mind all of the pain and anguish that came with it.

I continued to press the issue of her being stupid, insisting that she give me real, scientific, substantial, acceptable proof. She told me that she had flunked chemistry in a recent marking period, which she used as proof that she was stupid. This was an idea that was open to being attacked through examining it for a double standard.

I told her that I had flunked chemistry one marking period also, proof positive, I supposed, that I was stupid. She then did what most children and adolescents do when I turn their logic and conclusions about themselves toward myself or others. She objected vehemently.

I said to her, "You are not allowed to use a double standard around me. If a rule applies to you, it must also apply to me. You don't get to live by different rules than me or anyone else."

She insisted, quite emotionally, that she was not trying to live by any special rule that gave her advantages or privileges compared to others. I indicated back that this didn't matter. A double standard is a double standard, regardless of its purpose.

Laura had gotten mostly A's and B's throughout high school. She refused to see this as proof of intelligence, insisting that her classes were easy and that everyone in her group got good grades. I finally said that I wanted to give her an IQ test, figuring that the outcome of such a test would be pretty hard for her to argue with. I will admit that such a strategy was risky, as a low score would have been devastating. At the same time, having been around her during a number of sessions, I was convinced that she was quite bright. When I brought up the issue of an IQ test, she told me that she had taken some tests at her school, and she wondered if those scores would do. I had her mother sign a release of information, and several weeks later I got a copy of some achievement test scores.

Her scores ranged from a low of the eighty-eighth percentile, to a high of the ninety-seventh percentile, across the various parts of the test. She had no idea of how to interpret percentile scores, so I had her imagine a column of one hundred people her age, each one standing on the shoulders of the one below. I explained to her that the person at position number fifty would be the one with the average score, the person everyone else would be compared to. Anyone below him was below average, and anyone above him was above average. Her scores placed her at least thirty-eight positions above number fifty, and forty-seven positions above him on some parts of the test. She was, in that regard, way up in the clouds.

It was predictable that she refused to believe her own test results. I jokingly began to badger her with questions I use for people in her situation, due to my belief that the judicious use of humor with people who trust you can gently jar them out of their negative beliefs much faster than overly serious talk. I asked her who she bribed to give her these scores, since a dumb person couldn't score that high on an achievement test. I asked her if she paid someone else, someone very smart, to take her test for her. I asked her if she had a smart twin. I poked and prodded at her conclusions until she finally admitted that she was not dumb. As I recall it, she said, "OK, I'm not dumb. Does that make you happy?" While simply reading those words would imply that she was frustrated with me for pushing her in a direction that she did not want to go, I recall that she said them with humor and the type of relief you get when you finally put down a hundred-pound rock.

YOUR BRAIN IS FOOLING YOU

Who among us wants to admit that what we privately believe about ourselves isn't true? It is difficult enough for any of us to face our own real limits. If we don't look like models, and most of us don't, we can at least make the effort to take care of ourselves physically and dress the best that our budgets will allow. If we are not Einsteins, and most of us aren't, we can at least try to shoot for careers that we will find interesting. But why suffer from faults that don't exist?

It was hard for Laura to admit that she was not dumb. She held onto this idea even in the face of her good grades, because the faulty mental program running in her head had always whispered "dumb dumb dumb dumb dumb." These were, of course, her father's words and her boyfriend's words, shouted at her when they were drunk or angry or incapable of controlling themselves. The fact that their words could become her own thoughts constitutes one of the central horrors of cognitive depression. At some point she came to believe the bad things that people were saying to her. At some mysterious moment she began to hear their words in her own voice.

At first, Laura did not want to believe that her own thoughts were fooling her. She laughed at that notion when I opened it up. "How can your thoughts fool you?" she wanted to know. "Don't your thoughts tell you the truth?"

And yet, the more she allowed me to pick at her deeply held beliefs about herself, the more she was able to reject the hold they had on what she thought about herself and how she felt. Whenever she would begin to voice impossibly negative beliefs about herself as we continued in therapy, I would say to her, "Your brain is fooling you again. Where's your proof?" She would tell me that she *felt* ugly, that she *believed* she was ugly. I would counter that the only boys who flirted with her at school must be unattractive and undesirable. She would blush and tell me, "No, that's not true." Over the weeks I became quite insistent with her that anything she thought about herself had to be grounded in reality.

I remember her saying to me, "You just want me to think I'm perfect." And I said back to her, "No I don't. I just want you to be realistic about what you think about yourself. If you go around all day long beating yourself up for no real reason, the only way you can feel by the end of the day is depressed. There's nothing wrong with you accepting and working on your real faults. But there's no cure for your imaginary ones."

• • •

This is another story with a happy ending. Laura dumped her nasty-tempered boyfriend. She began to make plans to go to college and learned to overlook much of what her father had taught her to think about herself. I noticed that as she became more secure in herself, her clothing and makeup began to moderate. She began to move away from dressing in an overtly sexy manner to compensate for self-doubt or to attract young men whom she thought she would not attract unless she looked like a sex bomb. She came to accept that young men found her attractive, despite her pixy nose, and she learned to enjoy that fact.

I lost touch with her after she graduated. I understand that she did enroll in community college, with plans to eventually transfer to a four-year college. If we are to learn from her example, there are things we must be willing to do.

Three Plus Four Equals Seven

Laura's story illustrates an important point about structure: Be careful what you say to your child, because she might believe it. When you talk to your child, you are programming her mind. Laura, sadly enough, had been programmed by her father to hold hopeless beliefs about herself. On reflection, would any parent actually admit that his goal was to make his child feel stupid? Would you really want your child to think that mistakes are proof of inadequacy?

Listen mentally to what you are about to say to your child before you say it, particularly when you are angry. When you blow it and say something really mean, be quick to apologize. This teaches your child that you are willing to own up to your mistakes and helps her see that you didn't really mean what you said. You should understand, though, that regardless of apologizing we can only tell a child bad things about herself so many times before she begins to believe them.

Never Listen to Crazy People

I did my best to teach Laura that she must adamantly refuse to believe anything said to her by anyone whose desire it was to make her feel bad about herself. I ask children and teenagers to look at it this way: If I feel good about myself, I will have no need or desire to make someone else feel bad about themselves. This is, however, precisely the drive that motivates many of the people that your children will come into contact with during their lifetimes.

I tried to teach Laura that the people who want others to feel bad about themselves do so for one of two reasons. Either their emotional development got arrested at the point at which they feel superior to everyone around them (typical for four-year-olds and fourteen-year-olds), or they are so full of self-hatred that they cannot contain it. I told her that people who actively try to make others feel bad about themselves are displaying their own mental illness in public and that it is a mistake to take anything they say seriously. I told her to take bullies and other bad people as seriously as she might take some lunatic on the corner shouting that he has been sent here from the planet Zandar to enlighten the Earthlings.

HOW TO TELL IF YOUR CHILD BELIEVES HE IS MADE OF INFERIOR STUFF

There are no formal ground rules or tests to use to see if a child believes himself to be inferior. However, the following suggestions can help:

- Ask your child if he sometimes thinks others are "better" than him.
- Watch to see if your child allows others to dominate her or boss her around.
- Observe your child to see if she is hesitant to initiate interactions with others.
- Children who feel inferior are easily downed in arguments or discussions.
- Children who feel inferior are often hesitant to attempt anything new.
- It is hard for people who secretly feel inferior to admit their mistakes.
- It is hard for people who secretly feel inferior to laugh at themselves.
- Children and teenagers who feel inferior will, sooner or

later, make negative comparisons between themselves and others.

- Children and teenagers who feel inferior will be jealous of your attention toward others.

Should you become aware that your child or adolescent believes himself to be made of inferior stuff, you want to begin to talk to him on a regular basis about his thoughts. Here are some replacement beliefs, the types of things you want to convince your child to buy into instead of harboring hopeless beliefs:

- Your own thoughts are not necessarily true. You need proof for the bad things you think about yourself.
- If you have real proof about negative things about yourself, set about making a plan to change.
- There is nothing wrong with admitting the good things about you to yourself. No one is asking you to go on national TV and broadcast them.

Chapter 4

My Mistakes Are Proof That
I Am Worthless

I am currently working with Lyle, a nine-year-old boy who pitches an absolute falling-down fit every time he makes a mistake. It does not matter if the mistake is large or small, and it does not matter if he is at home or in public. In his mental mathematics:

mistake = stupid
and stupid = fit
therefore mistake = fit

One of the things that I learned about him was that he could not tolerate spilling anything. Whether it was milk or water or a soft drink, he would have a nuclear meltdown if he spilled something.

LYLE AND HIS DOUBLE STANDARDS

I tried talking to Lyle using the double standard technique, which we discussed in chapter 1. As you recall, many depressed people have one set of rules for themselves and another set for others. Typically, the rules that they try to apply to themselves are much more harsh and punitive than the ones they apply to others. I explained to Lyle that his brain had fooled him into believing that making a mistake was proof of something bad about him, but that other people could make exactly the same mistake and, in his eyes, still be OK. Our conversation went something like this:

ME: "Every time you spill a glass of water at home, you think you're stupid and you blow up, right?"

LYLE: "Yep."

ME: "Then every time I spill a glass of water it must mean I'm stupid too, right?"

LYLE: "No."

ME: "How can it mean that you're stupid if you spill a glass of water, but if I spill a glass of water I'm not stupid? I don't understand that."

LYLE: "I don't understand it either. That's just what it seems like."

ME: "If I spill a glass of water at my office it means I'm a stupid psychologist too, right?"

LYLE: "I don't think so."

ME: "Are you sure? It could be that I went to a special school for stupid psychologists."

LYLE: "Yeah, right!"

ME: "OK. But what if I were at your house and I spilled water out of the exact same glass that you spilled water out of before I got there? And what if it hit the exact same spot where you spilled your water? Wouldn't that mean I was stupid then, because I was at your house and I was using your glass and it hit the same spot?"

LYLE: "You're being stupid now, yourself!"

ME: "I suppose I am. But what does it really mean about me as a person if I spill a glass of water?"

LYLE: "It doesn't mean anything about you."

ME: "Then what could it really mean about you if you spill a glass of water?"

LYLE: "I don't know. I guess it couldn't really mean anything."

How do we go about saving Lyle from his own thoughts? If you had been there, you would have seen that he was trying to give me the obvious answer, the answer he probably realized that I wanted him to believe. But his heart wasn't really in it. He firmly believed that his mistakes meant that he was stupid, and try as I might, I could not budge him from that thinking.

• • •

It is obvious to anyone who stops and thinks about Lyle that he is headed for a life of unhappiness should he continue to think and act as he currently does. In order to help him, we have to think further about the notion of the human mental program.

One of the givens in human experience is that we fear what can harm us. Fear, being such a strong, visceral emotion, is necessary in terms of human evolution. Cavemen who were foolish enough to try to pet the saber-toothed tiger probably didn't survive long enough to pass along their genetic imprint. Their relatives who felt appropriate fear are among us today.

The more I listened to Lyle, though, the more I realized that the real issue was not that he simply didn't want to make mistakes. He had developed an almost unnatural fear of his mistakes because of the meaning he had placed on making mistakes.

Lyle is, unfortunately for him, a good example of the type of behavior you see when you combine depression and anxiety. He is anxious due to his fear of making mistakes, which he sees as proof of being stupid. Because he has proof that he is stupid, he is depressed. Because he is bound to make mistakes in his life, he is trapped in a vicious cycle.

DESENSITIZATION

It is certainly a good thing to talk to children about their fears. But if you really want a child or teenager to overcome his fears, he has to face them. One of the terms for this type of procedure is desensitization. It has been used for years to treat highly focused, specific phobias.

I once knew a woman, for example, who spent most of the summer cooped up in her house because she was desperately afraid of snakes. She had her husband build her an extra-wide concrete walkway from her driveway to her front step, so that she would be able to see any snake that might be lolling in the path from her car to her house. Because of some changes in her circumstances, she was forced to return to work full-time, which meant much more coming and going from home. It was making her a nervous wreck, because she was convinced that sooner or later she was going to encounter a snake.

I told her that one of the ways that we could begin to help her with her fear of confronting snakes was to desensitize her to seeing a snake. Her fear was so great at first that even imagining a snake would make her shudder. Not only could she not sit and watch a television show that featured snakes, she didn't even like to say the word.

I told her that I would soon begin to have a rubber snake on the floor of my office while we talked. She insisted at first that I keep it in a paper bag, which I obliged. Had I pushed her too rapidly, she would have left therapy, and nothing would have changed. Over a period of several sessions, she got to the point where she could sit comfortably in my office with the rubber snake on the floor. She could even make herself hold it, although not without great effort.

She finally agreed to meet me at the local nature center, where there was an exhibition room in which snakes were kept in glass enclosures set into the walls. When we first arrived, she could get no closer than twenty feet to one of the enclosures. I had her back out of the room slowly and do some breathing exercises to calm herself. Then I did my best to have her go back in.

Her first instinct was to say that treatment for that day was over and that we should just leave. I remained insistent, and over the next hour she made increasingly closer and closer approaches to the glass enclosures. The closest she could get was about five feet away.

She agreed to continue to go to the nature center with her husband, and over the course of the summer she began to report being able to come and go without any great difficulty. While she would never be the type of person who would want a python for a pet, her fears diminished to the point where her life seemed relatively normal.

• • •

What does all this have to do with Lyle? What do snakes have to do with making mistakes? The answer is that making a mistake, in particular spilling something, was Lyle's version of encountering a python in the wild.

One day when he was in my office with his mother, I placed an old coffee cup with water in it on my desk. As we began to talk, I slowly took the tip of my finger and began to push the cup toward the edge of my desk. He was riveted by the cup being pushed toward the edge, and he did not seem to hear a word I was saying. Rather, he began to bounce in his seat, bouncing faster and faster as the cup neared the edge.

"You're going to make a mess!" he finally shouted.

I continued to push the cup. I kept pushing it, searching for that point I knew would grip him even more, that point at which the cup would balance on the edge of the desk, leaning into thin air but not yet falling.

He continued to bounce, faster and faster until over went the cup. He shot off the couch as if catapulted. He ran to examine the water soaking into my carpet with the seriousness of an engineer examining a coolant leak at a nuclear power plant.

After we blotted up the water, I had Lyle sit at my desk and "accidentally" knock cups of water over the edge. The idea behind this was to desensitize him to mistakes just as the woman who was afraid of snakes had been desensitized to her fear. I knew that the first time he knocked over a cup he would be anxious and nervous. At the same time, I knew that if I had him knock twenty cups over, he would sooner or later come to see that it was "no big deal." I routinely teach children and teenagers to respond to their small mistakes by saying to themselves, "That's no big deal. I'll just fix it."

At first he resisted pushing off cups, saying that it was impossible for him to think "No big deal" to himself. He argued that it really was a big deal to spill stuff, although he couldn't tell me why. Finally he did knock a cup off, and then after some more talking another, and another. Somewhere along the way he managed to laugh. I began again to ask questions designed to probe his mental program, hoping that the process of spilling the water and seeing that it was, literally, no big deal, was beginning to alter his perceptions.

I know from experience that children and teenagers often believe something privately and only stop believing it once they speak their belief out loud and hear how ridiculous it sounds. In order to challenge his mental program, I continued to ask questions such as "How can something like knocking over a cup be proof that you are stupid?" I said to him that I was asking him these questions because I wanted us to reprogram his "meat computer," a description of the brain and the process that we were engaged in which he found amusing.

Young brains can be faulty devices when it comes to reality

testing, and most of the negative ideas they form about themselves are the end product of faulty thinking. Our children may be very bright for their age, but they don't have the life experience necessary to sort out good ideas from hopeless beliefs. While the Pentagon might listen to an eleven-year-old genius about building the next-generation nuclear bomb, would they take his advice on who to drop it on? I doubt it.

While some children can be relatively accurate observers of what is going on around them, they still have difficulty sorting out what to think about themselves. If my friend can hit a baseball, but I can't, what does that mean about me? If my classmate can add two-digit numbers and carry, but I can't, what does that mean about me? Children like Lyle frequently end up coming to faulty conclusions about themselves due to making mistakes, failing at something, being made fun of by their peers, having perfectionistic parents who chastise them too frequently, or for a host of other reasons. Being too young and naive to understand that their conclusions about themselves are faulty, they begin to adopt hopeless beliefs.

I explained to Lyle that we had to reprogram his meat computer. I told him that we had to reprogram it with new ideas that really made sense, ideas and thoughts and beliefs that wouldn't allow him to come to such faulty conclusions as believing that spilling water is a sign of being stupid.

You must be exceptionally persistent and direct when helping children and teenagers reprogram themselves. Their old programs have been running in the background twenty-four hours a day, seven days a week, for any number of years. Displacing their old programs with new programs requires persistence over everything else.

I persistently told Lyle that he *had* to begin to think that small mistakes, such as spilling things, were no big deal. I did not tell him just that I wanted him to think this way or that it would be

good for him to think this way. I told him that this was the way
that I thought, and that this was the way that everyone at my
house thought, and that because of this nobody got upset over little mistakes the way people did at his house. I insisted that not letting himself begin to think this way would keep him unhappy. I
asked him if, given a choice, he preferred to think in a way that
would make him unhappy or in a way that would make him happy.

I was quick to explain to him that he was still likely to encounter many, many other people who believed that mistakes were
terrible and horrible. Some of these people might even try to get
him to again believe that the little mistakes he made were proof of
something bad about himself. Those people, I told him, were as
trapped in their own faulty thinking as he had been in his.

I talked to Lyle and his parents about a set of replacement beliefs that I wanted all of them to use in their home. I had noticed
when I had him go through the exercise of spilling little cups of
water in my office that his mother seemed nervously transfixed.
Her only comment was, "I hope we don't have to practice that at
home."

It was clear that she did not like my answer, which was to explain to her that if she wanted him to stop blowing up about little
mistakes at home, he had to become desensitized to them. And
this meant turning over little cups of water on the kitchen counter
top or on her linoleum floor and saying to himself, "This is no big
deal. I'll just clean it up." I also told her that I wanted him to drop
an egg on the floor and drip mustard and ketchup on his shirt. I
thought she was going to have a heart attack.

In subsequent sessions I also taught his parents how to use a
technique with him that I refer to as The Two Brain Game. It is
important for people who are trying to reprogram their hopeless
beliefs to hear those hopeless beliefs at work as they think and to
learn to argue with them. In The Two Brain Game you ask the
child or teenager to pretend that his brain has been split in two.
One half is still running the faulty programs from the past, pro-

grams which are overly self-critical. The other half is running the new programs that you hope will replace the old programs.

When I play this game with children, and it admittedly goes over best with those under thirteen, I take the role of the part of the brain that is still running the old program. I ask the child I am working with to take the role of the part of his brain that is starting to use the replacement thoughts. The object of the game is to have the new replacement thoughts triumph over the old, depressive thoughts. It goes something like this:

ME: "You have to do everything perfectly. If you make mistakes, it means you are stupid or dumb or no good."

CHILD: "No it doesn't."

ME: "Yes it does. It will be terrible if you are not perfect."

CHILD: "That's not true. No one is perfect, and it is dumb to try to be."

ME: "But people won't like you if you're not perfect."

CHILD: "That's not true. Other people make mistakes too."

ME: "But some kids in your class are perfect. They're happy because they never make mistakes."

CHILD: "None of them is perfect, and they all make mistakes. They just don't worry about little mistakes."

ME: "But they should. Mistakes are horrible."

CHILD: "Some mistakes are horrible. But most of the mistakes we make are no big deal. All we have to do is clean up our mess."

The point here is to help the child escape his habitual ways of thinking. This type of exercise will go slowly at first, because the child's natural tendency will be to respond out of his old, faulty program, or it will be quite difficult for him to come up with the new, healthier answers. It is fine to give him hints along the way. You will find that, with practice, he will be much quicker to give reasonable answers.

Here are examples of the types of replacement beliefs I wanted Lyle to learn:

- Everyone on the planet makes at least one mistake every day. That's five billion mistakes daily. One more little mistake on your part is not going to matter.
- Most people admire others who own up to their own mistakes.
- We have the obligation to fix whatever it is we've messed up.
- Making mistakes does not mean that there is something bad or wrong about any of us.
- It makes no sense to treat little mistakes like something horrible has happened.
- There is no reason to blow up over a mistake. You still end up having to fix it. It is much better to fix it in a good mood than a bad mood.
- Your brain is fooling you if you think you can live a mistakeless life.
- You must apologize to the people inconvenienced by your mistake. Doing so is a sign of character and strength.

As nice as it is that Lyle responded positively in my office, his parents will have to follow through at home for months, if not longer, in order to reprogram his thought processes about mistake making and about what making mistakes means about his worth as a human being.

Not only will his parents have to remind him repeatedly that mistakes are no big deal, they will have to remind themselves. Once he, and they as a family, get to the point at which their automatic response to mistakes is to accept and fix what went wrong without an emotional scene, they will know that there is light at the end of the tunnel.

Chapter 5

No One Will Ever Like Me

I once knew a ten-year-old boy, Jeremy, who told me that he went to a middle school that had 300 students, counting him, and only one of them liked him. I said that minus his one friend, and minus himself, that meant that 298 of the students at his school did not like him. He nodded that this was indeed the case.

I decided that I would like to hear some of his "proof" for such an assertion. So I asked him to tell me what each of the other 298 children specifically had against him, assuming that he would back down as most kids would when faced with such a demand for proof. Instead, he began to go through his mental checklist.

"Johnny doesn't like me because we get in fights on the playground. Tommy doesn't like me because he likes Johnny. Donald doesn't like me because I wouldn't let him cut in line. Emily doesn't like me because she tried to steal my pencil and I took it back. Jermaine doesn't like me because he bumped into me and made me spill my drink and I told the teacher. . . ." And so on.

• • •

If you have a depressed child who has come to the belief that no one likes him, you know just how heartrending this can be. Every child's desire is to be loved and admired by his peers. Because of this, there is little else quite as sad as listening to a child tell you that he is an outcast.

Like most parents, you might feel the temptation to rush right in and say to your child, "There, there. This can't be so. How could it be possible that 298 children at your school do not like you?" It would be best to stop first and consider how such children think and behave, so that you get a clear understanding of how they have come to such conclusions.

One of the things that you will notice about children who claim that literally no one likes them is that they often fall into one of two patterns. The larger group, and the one that Jeremy fell into, is composed of children who are stiff or reserved or not outgoing. Often these children are unsure of themselves or have difficulty laughing at themselves. They frequently feel rejected by children who laugh at them but who, in reality, are not attempting to reject them.

The other, much smaller group of children who voice complaints about not being liked are the class clowns. They set about entertaining others and making them laugh, out of the belief that it is the only way to be liked. At first they confuse being laughed at with being liked. At some point they realize that even though others laugh at them, they are rarely included in the group. Their peers avoid being around them because it leads to trouble with the teachers. Others view them as funny but obnoxious. The most dramatic and, paradoxically, the funniest of the class clowns are often avoided because, while they have learned to entertain, they've rarely learned how to actually interact. You can't have a real conversation with someone else when you're hogging the stage.

You will hear a number of other beliefs when you talk to children who claim that no one likes them. They believe, for example, that not only do others dislike them, no one will ever like them. They assume that the reason others do not like them has nothing to do with their own behavior. They believe that people who don't like them are snotty and stuck up. They assume, as did Jeremy, that everyone at their school knows them, even though they have had interactions with only a fraction of the total student body. They are paranoid in their logic, vigilant and watchful. They assume that the next insult is just around the corner.

WHEN YOU ENCOUNTER REAL PROOF

The real problem is that, quite often, children like Jeremy are right. No one likes them. At some point I always send the child making this kind of complaint back into the waiting room so that I can talk to his parents. The parents all too often describe a pattern in which their child does not get calls from other children inviting him over. Or they tell me that their child initiates phone calls to others, but everyone always has an excuse about why they can't come over. They frequently say that their child is never included among the kids his age roaming about the neighborhood having fun, is often alone on the playground at school, doesn't get invited to parties, doesn't get chosen to be on sports teams, and so on. You don't have to think about this very long to understand why it would have a depressing effect on the child's mood and leave his self-concept in tatters.

The first step in helping a child who complains that no one likes her is to verify the claim. If you really do not know whether or not your child is being universally rejected, you need to find out more about her world. Go to her school and ask her teachers if it is true that she is being ignored by others. Make sure to watch her in group settings to see if she is attempting to talk to others or if others are attempting to talk to her. If you have close friends in the neighborhood, ask them what the other children say about her. If you find that the other children are avoiding your child, you have two types of inventories you must take.

The first type of inventory involves taking a close look at your child's physical appearance. Does he dress in a way (or do you dress him in a way) that makes him stand out from the other children? One sad fact about social hierarchies is that children and teenagers can get away with dressing in a highly individualized style if they are already popular or if they have the self-confidence to pull it off smoothly. If not, the other children will automatically view your child's differences as negative.

I've often told a story about a young man I met a number of years ago. He had not yet reached puberty and was about age eleven. His mother complained to me that he had no friends and that the other children at his school made fun of him and were mean to him.

All you had to do was look at him to see why. He had an exceptionally odd haircut that laid on his head at strange angles, considerably predating the "bed head" look that is popular today. His pants were too short for the style at that time, and he wore an old man–type of shirt. Plus, he always had grease under his fingernails. He was a mechanical genius who loved nothing more than taking apart and rebuilding the small engines his father had given him to practice on.

His mother became outraged when I told her that she needed to make sure that he dressed differently, had a haircut more in keeping with the style of his peers, and kept his fingernails clean. Sad to say, she didn't bring him back to see me.

The second type of inventory involves listening to your child talk so that you can find out how he attempts to interact with others. I recently talked to an eight-year-old boy who was having some social difficulties with the other boys. Fortunately, his was another case in which the main reason for being rejected was readily evident. He spent all of his free time talking about the band the Spice Girls. He wanted to know who my favorite Spice Girl was, and he told me about his Spice Girl posters. He asked me if I knew the titles to any of their songs.

Here's the problem: The Spice Girls had fallen off the face of the earth about a year earlier. Even at the height of their popularity, they were primarily a band that my girl patients were nuts over and that my boy patients couldn't care less about. The fact that he was trying to talk to the other boys about this band, at this particular time, was guaranteed to place him at odds with his peers. One of the first things we talked about was that he certainly had a right to like any band and any type of music he wanted to like, but it was also smart to know what the other boys were into.

It is exceptionally important to observe your child talking to other children so that you can tell if he acts as mature as his peers. I knew a boy a number of years ago who, for lack of a better description, had to reduce all interactions with other boys down to burps and farts.

I used to observe him at soccer games. Before or after the games, he would make his way into a group of guys who were standing around talking about the game, or about school, or other social events. He didn't really have the emotional maturity to talk with the other children at their level. Somewhere in there, usually like clockwork, he would burp in an attempt to make everyone laugh. Or, he would blow on his arm. Or, he would do that thing that boys are genetically programmed to do in which they put one hand under their armpit and crank their other arm up and down, making what kids refer to as "arm farts."

The curative actions that a parent can take once it is clear that her child is being socially rejected are rarely as simple as changing how he dresses, although that is important. It is much more important to teach your child the types of social skills which will help him become more acceptable to his peers. Keep in mind that you will probably do this teaching amidst your child's protests that it is not fair, that he does not need to change, and that it is the other kids who should be making changes. It is important that you be persistent and set structure. Let your child know that improving his social skills is not optional. It is mandatory.

TEACHING CHILDREN TO COMMUNICATE

For starters, your child or teenager will stand little chance of fitting into a group of her peers unless she knows how to initiate and hold conversations. The key to this is to teach her that she must ask others about themselves and their interests, prior to talking about herself. The only way to practice this is for you to have conversations with her on a regular basis until it is clear that she can converse with relative ease. Do not be swayed by her insistence that she already understands what you are asking her to do and that she will do it at school or out in the neighborhood. Have her practice with you.

On the other hand, she may tell you that she does not know what to talk to other people about. Listen closely, because she may be telling the truth. Not all children have an automatic sense of what to talk to others about. It never would have occurred to Jeremy, our young man who was disliked by his 298 peers, to ask a Martian what life was like on Mars. He just didn't think to ask people about themselves. One of your first jobs may be to help your child devise a mental list of topics that most kids her age are talking about. I should add that you should not be fooled by the fact that your child might be very good at coming up with things to talk to adults about. Some children and teens can talk to adults with ease but freeze solid in front of kids their own age.

The list of things to talk to your peers about, once you think about it, could be nearly endless. You can ask others about their favorite music group or their favorite songs. What is your favorite brand of clothing? Where do you like to go on weekends? Have you seen any good movies lately? What is your favorite sport? What do you hope to become one day? Where would you like to go to college?

The list will vary depending upon your child's age and sex and, to some extent, where you live. Some of the things that ten-year-old boys from the country like to talk about might not interest their city peers, and vice versa. Teenagers from Toronto may be gaga over hockey, whereas teenagers from Miami may be nuts about baseball.

Knowing Who Not to Talk To

There are several risks associated with having your child attempt to start conversations in order to improve her social skills and her social standing with her peers. We all know that children and teenagers can be cruel. Such children may respond to your child's attempts with mockery or with put-downs. Given this, it is smart to have a strategy for whom to start conversations with and how to handle put-downs and insults.

A painful aspect of developing a strategy is to be aware of your child's social standing among her peers. If she is indeed being rejected by almost everyone, if she is at the bottom of the pecking order in her class, it would be foolish for her to attempt to start conversations with children who are at the top of the pecking order. She is likely to be rejected or, at best, treated coolly by them.

In addition, it is not a smart strategy to attempt to start a conversation with someone when they are hanging out with their own group. Your child would only seem like an intruder. You, as the parent, will be smart to remember that the purpose of a clique is to exclude others. Sending a child like Jeremy to school with the intent of trying to try to talk to a dominant member of his class would be like sending him on a kamikaze mission. It is better instead to ask your child to give you a list of names of classmates who are not members of an exclusive group. Your best strategy is to go to her school and ask her teacher which children seem the most friendly and approachable. Many teachers, on learning of concerns like these, will arrange for your child to work one-on-one with a friendly child and will be willing to observe her behavior and give you some feedback.

There are additional reasons that attempts to make conversations with others might fail. If your child has not had enough practice, her attempts to start a conversation could seem forced or artificial. It could be that your child is doing as she should when making the attempt, but the child she is trying to talk to does not have the social skills to engage in conversation. Or your child might run into a child who just doesn't want to talk to anyone to begin with. Again, this is why it is best to have a strategy on whom to try to talk to and whom to avoid.

Eye Contact

Another skill that your child will need if she is being rejected by others is knowing how to make eye contact.

Eye contact is a funny subject. Some subgroups in Western culture value it, while others do not. My own bias is to believe that you have little chance of being successful in mainstream American culture if you do not know how to make eye contact while interacting with others. A rule that I ask parents to adopt with children and teenagers who need to work on eye contact is to say to them, "I cannot hear you without eye contact." Be sure to stick by this rule.

Facial Expression

Facial expression is just as important as eye contact, and your child needs to understand what her facial expression looks like as she is making eye contact. None of us is truly aware of what our faces look like as we talk, even though your child is likely to insist that she knows exactly, precisely, and without any possible room for error, what her face looks like as she talks. Jeremy actually made excellent eye contact, if you were not concerned about what the rest of his face was doing. His raised eyebrows, lack of blinking, and tightly pursed lips made him look as if he were expecting you to try to pull his skull out through his nose at any second. Worse, even, was the fact that as he talked, he tried to smile. But he smiled with his worried eyebrows in full-tilt fearful mode. I have asked his parents to make sure that they give him gentle but honest feedback on his facial expressions and to make sure that they practice, using role plays, over and over until he looks comfortable.

You may also need to give your child feedback on other things, such as voice volume, clarity, and speaking rate. Others may not find your child to be socially desirable if he mumbles, speaks too quickly or too slowly, or speaks too softly or too loudly. Be sure to give such feedback gently and in small doses. No child can cope with the idea that he does everything wrong.

GETTING JEREMY TO ACCEPT WHO HAS TO CHANGE

To return to Jeremy: His parents had to come to understand his thought process. As with most kids who assert that no one likes them, his thinking had a paranoid streak. Children who have such a streak are often keen observers of who said or did what. Like real paranoids, however, they almost always assign the wrong motive to the other person's behavior. Jeremy's parents had to repeat to him, over and over, that it was not really likely that everyone at his school disliked him. Still more difficult, they had to convince him that it was quite unlikely that everyone at his school was even aware of his existence. He finally admitted this when I challenged him one day to name all of the people at his school.

There were two ideas that we had to get this young man to understand and accept before he could begin to feel better. Both were understandable enough, but neither was initially acceptable to him. The first, and more important, was that if someone is disliked by literally everyone in his class, it is likely that he is doing something drastically wrong. He may not be doing it on purpose. It is likely that he is not even aware that he is doing anything wrong. But, somewhere along the line, he is making some large error.

Second, the person who is out of favor with literally all of his peers is the one who has to change, not his peers. Telling this boy that he had to make changes if he wanted others to like him sent him into fits of righteous indignation.

Jeremy began to make improvements only after I repeatedly forced him to see that his way of thinking was unrealistic. I had him play The Two Brain Game with me many times, during which I pretended to be part of his mind and said things that were so unrealistic that they forced him into coming up with realistic thoughts so he could argue with me. Ultimately, this began to help him reject his beliefs about being universally disliked. It went something like this:

> ME: "Those other kids at school hate us. Every single one of them."
>
> JEREMY: "That's not true. All of them don't even know us."
>
> ME: "Sure they do. Everyone knows us."
>
> JEREMY: "That's not possible."
>
> ME: "Then why is everybody so mean to us every day?"
>
> JEREMY: "Everybody is not mean to us every day. Some people are. But not everybody."
>
> ME: "Then they should change the way they act toward us!"
>
> JEREMY: "They're not going to change. We have to learn to ignore people who aren't nice to us."
>
> ME: "But nobody is ever going to be nice to us."
>
> JEREMY: "Everybody won't be. But we have to do better at trying to talk to other people too. They won't like us if we don't try to talk to them about stuff they like."

You can see the direction this is headed in. The more I continued to voice paranoid, unrealistic concerns, the more Jeremy was forced into bringing me back to reality. Hopefully, by playing such games, your own child will learn to bring herself back to reality also.

I should add that The Boy with 298 Enemies, as I once privately thought of Jeremy, became The Boy with a Small Group of Friends. His parents learned to nip his paranoid thinking in the bud by doing such things as asking him for his proof and having him play The Two Brain Game with them. While he hated doing the role plays in which he had to make eye contact and talk to others about what they were interested in, his parents did find that over time his social skills improved. He began to smile more readily, he laughed at jokes, and he was more able to take part in a conversation.

Jeremy's parents had to work steadily to reprogram how he thought, given that he was so paranoid. Here is a list of the types of things that we tried to get him to think, instead of falling back into his old ways of thinking:

- It is not likely that you are either universally liked or universally hated. Most kids have a few close friends and a few people who don't like them.
- It is not possible that everybody at your school knows you. It is not even likely that everyone in your grade knows you.
- It is not possible that everyone in your class needs to change. If you want people to like you, you have to work hard to make yourself likable.
- It is not likely that other people are talking about you. They have other things to do.
- It is smart to know who to try to talk to. Avoid unfriendly people.
- Avoid the temptation of trying to get others to like you by making them laugh. You have to earn friendship by being involved with others. This means asking them questions about themselves and showing them that you care about them.

Chapter 6

The "F" Word

I will admit to you publicly that my own children use the "F" word on me. Usually it's at home, but sometimes it's in public. It's typically when I have made them mad or when I've done something that disappoints them. They will step right up to me, look me right in the eye, and say, "Dad, that's not *fair*."

Like most kids, my own have been through the phases in which they believe that if they do not get what they want, something is not fair. This is a normal stage and nothing to worry about.

I have no quarrel with parents teaching their children and teenagers to act fairly toward others. I have attempted to teach my own children to be fair-minded individuals. The problem comes when children begin to believe that just because they are pleasant, act nice, and treat others fairly, others are guaranteed to act similarly toward them.

I remember my own first big lesson in the realities of human nature. I was five and was at the school Halloween party. My mother had me go up on stage to compete for best costume with the other kids my age, and I won. My prize was a big tin of butter mints. When I got back to my seat, I opened up the tin and showed them to her. She nodded toward the little boy sitting beside me and said, "Ask him if he'd like one."

I had yet to have one myself. But, having been raised in a sharing and fairness-oriented family, I moved the tin toward him and asked him if he'd like one. The little barbarian stuck his hand in there and grabbed a whole fistful.

Why am I so concerned with this fairness issue? Am I advising you to teach your children to not worry about being fair? The answer is no. I am strongly of the opinion that it is good for us to teach our children to be fair. But I am just as strong in my opinion that it is important to teach them how to recognize who to extend their fairness to. Let me tell you why.

Years ago I worked with depressed adults. I learned that an alarming number of them believed that they had spent their lives being more fair to others than others had been to them. Adults trapped in a fairness-based depression tend to view the world as a barren place that withholds rewards due the really good for being good. They are frequently strong in their assertion that they have treated their spouse or life partner better than they have been treated in return. Many of them also have lengthy lists of other significant people in their lives with whom they claim the scales have always been unbalanced.

They seem to believe that they are the ultimate judge of whether or not others are fair to them. In this regard, if they extend a favor to you, even if you do not want it, they already have it mapped out in their mind what you must extend back to them. If you do not offer what they anticipated that you would offer, then you have treated them unfairly.

They especially tend to have a hard time around people who do not feel a need to be nice or fair. If they were smart and had their wits about them, they would just walk away from these unpleasant types. But instead of walking away from truly unfair individuals, one of the deep aspects of their mental program goes into overdrive: I will *make* you be fair to me through the force of my own fairness toward you. If you wonder if such a twisted viewpoint really exists, just ask yourself how many people you've known who've stuck like glue to boyfriends or girlfriends, husbands or wives, who treated them like dirt.

This is the circular thinking that goes along with fairness-based depression:

- It is not fair that I treat you better than you treat me.
- It is your treatment of me that causes me to be depressed.
- I will not feel better until you change.
- Because you will not change, I will remain depressed and secretly angry with you.
- Even though I am angry with you, I will still treat you better than you treat me.
- It is not fair that I treat you better than you treat me. (And we're back where we started.)

Because many depressed adults think this way, their strongest fantasy is that one day the people who have wronged them will admit that they treated them poorly, apologize profusely, and promise never to do it again. You do not want your child to grow up thinking this way.

In order to help children and teenagers avoid this particular trap, we have to listen to them closely to learn to what extent they actually expect others to return their fairness and to what extent they believe that by being nice they can somehow force the truly unfair individuals to become fair to them. It is quite difficult for children and teenagers who are depressed over fairness issues to move beyond the viewpoint that everyone else should change. And I will admit that I meet many depressed children and teenagers who are genuinely fair and nice and who sound to me to be in unbalanced relationships with some of their less pleasant peers.

The first, and most major, hint that your child is caught up in a fairness-based depression is when you hear her complain repeatedly that others are not being fair to her. You then have to ask in a very direct, straightforward manner if she believes that she treats everyone better than they treat her and if she believes that she can make those people be nice to her by continuing to be nice to them.

Take Aaron, for example. He is a quiet, friendly seven-year-old who is generally liked by most of his classmates. He doesn't fit any convenient stereotypes. He wears glasses and is studious, but is also a good soccer player. His mother reported to me that he was beginning to tell her that he didn't want to go to school and that he was also beginning to stay inside more than normal. He struck her as being depressed. She took him to see his pediatrician, who suggested that some talk therapy might get to the root of the issue.

The root of the issue emerged pretty quickly. Aaron's best friend, James, had begun to develop a close friendship with a third boy, Ramon. When Aaron's friend and this boy were together, they would make fun of Aaron, or call him names, or tell him that they didn't want him sitting by them at lunch. When James was not with Ramon, he acted his normal self. Aaron's chief complaint: "It's not fair that he treats me mean when he's with Ramon, but tries to be my friend when it's just me and him."

SKUNK TRAINING

While not universally true, many depressed children and adolescents have a pleasant, but somewhat dependent personality style. They are sometimes too open to accepting the harsh criticism of some of their more antisocial peers, and they integrate the negative things their peers say into their own thinking about themselves. Aaron was this way.

There are particular types of children whom boys like Aaron have trouble with. Take, for example, your basic steamroller playground bully. He's too busy having fun using others as objects for his enjoyment to spend any time in self-reflection or self-doubt. Or take the overly self-assured, narcissistic child who tends to be highly judgmental of others. Such children are often so sure that they are not lacking in any way that to entertain the type of self-doubt seen in boys like Aaron would be impossible. Neither bullies nor narcissists are prone to self-reflection, and neither are particularly open to listening to what others attempt to tell them about themselves. They don't even stop to think about whether or not they are being fair to others.

Boys like Aaron are exactly the opposite: often too critical in their self-assessments, too concerned with being nice to everybody, and too willing to have their own self-worth defined by others.

When I encounter preadolescent children who strike me as being depressed due to being picked on or being put down by others, I frequently engage them in what I call "skunk training." Skunk training goes like this: I ask them if they have ever seen a real skunk. I tell them that if they saw a skunk and didn't know what it was, they might think that it was a pretty, fuzzy little animal that was a lot like a cat. Then I tell them about the campground I went to as a teenager. Animals from the outlying woods would come into the campsites looking for food. One summer a little kid who was there with his family tried to pick up a skunk that had wandered in looking for food. I doubt that it was a mistake that he ever made again. That day he not only learned how to recognize skunks, but he also learned everything he would ever need to know about their nature.

I go on to tell these children that there are human skunks in the world, a description that they tend to enjoy. We talk about how sometimes these human skunks can look and act pretty friendly, but that if you forget what they are, they will spray you. I should warn you that kids caught in the potty-humor phase (mainly boys) tend to have great fun with this idea.

We talk about how human skunks spray you when you drop your guard. They do it primarily with words, by calling names or using verbal put-downs. They are usually smart enough and mean enough to do this in front of other children, so that their words have the maximum impact upon their target.

I also remind children that human skunks, unlike real skunks, tend to run in herds. There are many skunks whose nature does not make itself known unless they are with the herd. You might be able to interact with them quite pleasantly one on one, but you'll find yourself being sprayed once they are around their friends and you come into the vicinity.

The main point in skunk training is this: You must identify who it is in your class or your neighborhood who is prone to act like a skunk. You are not to tell him that he is a skunk. This would do no good at all and would make you a favored target. Your strategy is to simply ignore each and every word that a skunk says to you, regardless of how nice or friendly it might sound. You know that sooner or later, if you drop your guard and try to be friendly back to them, you're going to end up needing a bath.

We can also talk to postadolescents about skunks, but it has to be in a different way. I will often tell a depressed teenager about how I train little kids to recognize skunks, and they will in turn tell me that they know some skunks their own age. My general advice to teenagers about skunks is to ask them whether or not they should listen to what a skunk teenager says when they know the skunk's goal is to make them feel bad about themselves. I ask the teenager I'm working with to remember the central fact about bullies and sociopaths—their goal is to make others feel bad about themselves. Given this, it remains best to ignore everything that they have to say. If you allow them to hurt your feelings, they win the game.

IT'S NOT NICE TO SAY "NO"

Another aspect of always wishing to be fair or nice is the belief that it is not nice to say "No" to anyone. Most children will be able to tell you that it is OK for them to say "No," but don't be fooled by this answer. When it comes to determining if your child is really able to be assertive and to stand up for herself, it is much better to observe what she does than to listen to what she tells you she believes.

Many children are hesitant to say "No" to the requests of their peers because they think that if they do, their peers won't like them anymore. You can probably tell if your child or teenager falls into this category by watching her with her friends or by listening to her talk about her friends. Does she complain about doing things for her friends that she does not really want to do, such as loaning them money or clothes or providing them with transportation? Does she outwardly agree with what they are saying when you know for a fact that she thinks otherwise? Is she easily led? If so, it may be useful to do some assertiveness training with her to help her overcome her fear of saying what she really wants to say.

You may wish to talk to your child or teenager about the three roles she can assume when responding to her peers. The first role, the "doormat," is characterized by making one or two feeble attempts to be assertive before caving in. I role play this with kids. If teenagers will role play with you, they will learn how to be assertive more quickly than if you just talk. However, teens are often reticent about role playing, and you have to use your judgment on how yours will best pick up new skills. The role play, in which I am in the doormat role, might go like this:

> FRIEND: "I really need you to take me to my boyfriend's house after school. His car isn't working, so he can't pick me up.

> DOORMAT: "I don't know. I might have some other stuff I
>   have to do."
> FRIEND: "Like what? Couldn't you do it after you give me a
>   ride?"
> DOORMAT: "Well, I don't know."
> FRIEND: "Oh come on. You know I'd give you a ride if I had a
>   car."
> DOORMAT: "OK. I guess I can do it."

You can see that I am hoping desperately that my friend will realize that I really don't want to give her a ride to her boyfriend's
house. However, she apparently has her own agenda, and she did
not take the hint. In the end I agreed to give her a ride. Ultimately,
this teaches my friend that if she leans on me just a little bit, I will
cave in and do what she wants.

The second role, the "monster," is the exact opposite of the
doormat. The person in the doormat role attempts to protect herself by dropping hints so that the person who is asking the favor
will realize that she is trying to decline. The person in the monster
role acts in a more brutal manner:

> FRIEND: "Could you give me a ride to my boyfriend's house
>   after school? His car is broken, and I really need you to take
>   me over there."
> MONSTER: "What do I look like to you, the taxi service?"
> FRIEND: "Oh come on. I really need you to help me. I'd help
>   you."
> MONSTER: "Like I'm certain. You seem to think I'm your
>   magic carpet or something."

At some point my friend's lights will finally go on, but before they
do, it is likely that my sarcastic comments will be hurtful. It would
be much better for me to remain in what I refer to as the "middle
ground" role.

I train children and teenagers that the middle ground role of assertiveness has certain rules and strategies. Responding in the middle ground role means that each person has the right to answer someone else's question or request honestly. If you answer in a way that is honest, moral, and ethical, and the other person blows up or gets angry, it is not your fault and it is not your job to try to fix it. You have the right to tell the truth.

To successfully claim the middle ground role, you must be willing to repeat yourself. A role play might sound like this:

FRIEND: "I really need for you to give me a ride to my boyfriend's house after school today. His car is broken, and he can't pick me up."

REPEATER: "I'm sorry, I can't do it today."

FRIEND: "Why not?"

REPEATER: "Because I have some other plans for myself after school."

FRIEND: "Couldn't you just run me over there and then go do your things?"

REPEATER: "No, I'm afraid not."

FRIEND: "But I'd take you if you were in my situation."

REPEATER: "It's like I said, I can't do it today."

FRIEND: "But I thought we were friends."

REPEATER: "We are. But like I said, I can't do it today."

FRIEND: "You never told me why you can't."

REPEATER: "It's like I said, I just can't do it today."

FRIEND: "Jeez."

My friend is getting pushy and is using several ploys to try to get me off of the middle ground. By questioning our friendship, she is trying to make me feel guilty. She is trying to make me explain what it is I have to do after school, an explanation that I owe to no one. At the end, she is obviously angry with me, perhaps hoping that I will sense her anger and try to patch things up by giving in.

My strategy instead was to be willing to politely repeat myself.

There is a humorous game I use to teach assertiveness to children and teenagers who are clearly hesitant to say what they really think. It entails pointing out something in my office, like my desk clock or one of the prints on my wall, and asking the child or teen if it isn't the best one he has ever seen. I know at some point in the game he will grow bolder and begin to tell me no, that the object I am referencing is not the best one he has ever seen. Typically, the longer we play, the more relaxed he will become about stating his opinion in a kind, but assertive manner. For example:

ME: "See this pen I'm using? Don't you think it is the best pen in the whole world?"

CHILD: "It probably is."

ME: "And how about this little tissue holder? Don't you think it is the nicest one in the whole world?"

CHILD: "It's really nice."

ME: "But isn't it probably the nicest one in the whole world? None better, right?"

CHILD: "I don't know."

ME: "You know I never accept 'I don't know' as an answer."

CHILD: "I don't really think it is the nicest one in the whole world."

ME: "Then how about these shoes I'm wearing? Wouldn't you like to have a pair just like them that you could wear to school?"

CHILD: "No."

ME: "Why not? They're really nice shoes."

CHILD: "I'd look stupid in them. Kids my age don't wear those."

ME: "Then what about my watch? Isn't it the best one you've ever seen?"

CHILD: "No!"

If during the game the child becomes derisive or insulting, I reel him in and let him know that his job is to tell the truth, but to do so in a way that is polite as well as honest. In general, most children seem to enjoy the game, and they learn from it.

Teaching your child or teenager not to fall into fairness traps will serve him well over time. If your child is to understand that he does not have to believe the bad things said to him by others or the bad things he could come to think about himself when mistreated by others, he needs to learn certain replacement thoughts and beliefs from you. In no particular order, they are:

- Judge yourself based on what you do well, not on what you do poorly.
- Listening to people who want you to feel bad about yourself is a waste of time.
- It is OK to say "No."
- If you tell the truth in a way that is honest, moral, and ethical, and others blow up, it is not your fault.
- Just because someone asks something of you or expects something of you, does not mean you have to do it.
- You are not the source of happiness for others. They must find their own happiness.

Chapter 7

I Can't Live Without This Person

Teenagers have always come under intense peer pressure to be partnered in serious relationships. While the urge to hook up with someone in a semipermanent relationship is a normal developmental state, the pressure to make such hookups today seems to be much more serious than in previous generations. I refer to these intense relationships as miniature marriages.

A miniature marriage, by definition, is a highly formalized union between a boy and a girl, usually between the ages of fourteen and eighteen. The rules of the miniature marriage are that, excepting your partner, you do not look at another person of the opposite sex, and you do not talk to another person of the opposite sex. Years ago, if you flirted with someone's boyfriend or girlfriend, you might get yelled at or possibly threatened. Today, in extreme cases, crossing over into the boundaries of someone else's miniature marriage can get you shot.

Many of these young couples have their honeymoons planned before they can even drive. Because they believe that they are getting married one day, it logically follows that having sex is OK. All hell breaks loose when these miniature marriages fail, as they are almost always fated to do.

Why do we see so many of these miniature marriages today? The reasons appear to be numerous. It is not at all uncommon for both partners in the miniature marriage to be from chaotic homes or broken homes where there is no closeness between the parents or between parent and child.

Today it takes two parents working to provide the lifestyle that in previous years could be had with one parent working. When there are no parents around, or when the parents are so worn out from work that they do not take the time to talk and teach and interact, children and teenagers are forced to raise themselves. Their miniature marriages provide them with the structure and order and routine which are missing in their family lives. One sixteen-year-old girl I knew, whose mother died suddenly and whose father was always at the office, latched onto a boy with few skills or prospects who was equally lonely and could be easily dominated. She made him buy her a ring, and made him buy her a dog. He had to be at her house every night at seven to walk the dog with her. Instant family.

Earlier we talked about Joe, the teenager who was brought sobbing into my office after his girlfriend had broken up with him. He was very clear about the idea that he could not live without his girlfriend, and he believed the loss of his miniature marriage was too much for him to take. Once you begin to understand how Joe thought about his relationship, you can quickly understand why he was such an emotional mess. His thinking about his miniature marriage serves to illustrate the type of faulty thinking that leads teenagers into deep difficulties:

- My relationship with my girlfriend is more important to me than school or career.
- My relationship with my girlfriend is more important to me than my parents.
- My relationship with my girlfriend is more important to me than my friends.

- My relationship with my girlfriend is equal in importance to a real, legal marriage.
- My relationship will never end.
- My girlfriend is the only woman I will ever be interested in.
- My girlfriend can meet all of my emotional, spiritual, and physical needs.
- My girlfriend should never find other males attractive.

You only have to think briefly about these beliefs, these mental programs, to understand the pressures they can generate in a teenager's life. Like most of the faulty thinking that is behind depression, it was not easy to get Joe to let go of these beliefs and replace them with more rational thinking.

For example, Joe apparently liked to believe that his girlfriend, when they were still together, would never look at other males and find them to be attractive. The idea that she might do so would leave him angry and upset. He had a clear double standard. I asked him if he ever secretly took a glance at young women other than his girlfriend when they were still going together. He admitted that he had. He resisted the idea, though, that glancing at other people and finding them attractive was entirely normal. He did not like it when I told him that it was a perfectly normal stage of human development for young men and women to find themselves attracted to numerous other people. I had to tell Joe that his insistence that any future girlfriend would never be allowed to look at another male was contrary to the laws of human nature.

• • •

What should you do when you realize that your teenager is in a miniature marriage? This is a more terrifying question than it may at first seem. It is merely within the realm of the obnoxious for your teenager to walk around with his own cordless phone grafted to his ear or pagers and cell phones with voice mail and digital messaging hanging like strange fruit from his belt because his miniature wife insists that she must have twenty-four-hour access to him. It moves considerably beyond the realm of the obnoxious when you consider the possibility of early pregnancy. Additionally, the majority of teenagers I see who want to kill themselves are in that state of mind because a miniature marriage has collapsed.

The best strategies for preventing a miniature marriage start with prevention. I worked with a family several years ago whose daughter, age sixteen, was on the telephone for three to four hours nightly with her boyfriend. This was a bright girl who was capable of getting grades in the A and B range, but who was getting mainly D's. When your whole evening is devoted to the telephone, it is no wonder that academic performance will suffer. Parents should hold a firm line about telephone use, especially on school nights.

Given that most teenagers are at home at night, the telephone is the breeding ground for miniature marriages. When you hold your teenager to no more than an hour of phone time after school, you make it harder for miniature marriages to sprout. It goes without saying that parents should firmly resist having their teenagers wear pagers unless the parent has a clear need to be able to reach the teenager. If you fail to do so, you will find that your child is being paged at all hours of the day or night, often by people you have never met.

I have similar doubts about the instant messaging craze that is currently so popular on computers. I know teenagers who spend hours each night sending and receiving "I.M." I know one girl who sits at her computer typing I.M. messages while she is on the phone making conference calls with her friends. She has call waiting, call forwarding, caller I.D., pager forwarding, whatever. Were you to look at all of the technological communication solutions she employs so that others may reach her, you would think that she was the chairperson of Ford Motor Company or an emergency trauma surgeon instead of a fifteen-year-old with an overheated social calendar.

Regarding the girl whose grades were suffering and who was on the phone for hours each night: What I eventually found out was that her boyfriend, who went to the same school she went to but who tended to skip a lot of classes, was calling her each day at almost the exact time she arrived home from school. He demanded to know where she had been if she was late and who she had talked to at school each day. He would get enraged if he thought she had talked to any males. He insisted that she wear a pager, which he paid for, so that he could track her down at any time. When she would try to get off of the phone, he would tell her that she didn't really love him and that he intended to kill himself.

By the time I saw this girl, she was distraught with fear that her boyfriend would kill himself and that it would be her fault. I talked her into telling her parents what was going on, so that her parents could alert the boy's parents about his constant suicide threats and his obsessive relationship. While he apparently denied making suicide threats, the calls did cease. Eventually, as in most miniature marriages, they went separate ways. My guess is this boy will grow up to be the type of man who grills his wife about who she is talking to or looking at, wants her to wear a pager and carry a cell phone so that he can always find her, and spends a large portion of his income hiring private detectives to follow her around.

HOPELESS BELIEFS AND MINIATURE MARRIAGES

The root of such jealous behavior is, of course, insecurity. It is grounded in one of the hopeless beliefs that we examined: "I am made of inferior stuff." Young men and young women who become obsessive in relationships have minds that are flooded with negative fantasies that their partners are cheating or secretly finding others to be more attractive. Their own thinking tells them that they are not good enough to really hold their partner's interest, and eventually they settle on coercive methods, such as suicide threats or threats to beat up anyone who might look at their partner, to make sure that their partner does not leave them. While such young people believe that the key to happiness is to just be with their partner twenty-four hours per day, the only real key to happiness will come when they confront themselves about their poor self-concept.

As for the girl who feared that her boyfriend would commit suicide, our work eventually centered around her beliefs that it was not nice to say no and that she was responsible for other people's happiness. I talked to her at length about how it was not in her best interest to enter into relationships in which she was going to attempt to "fix" her intended partner. Like many good teenagers, she felt responsible for her boyfriend and wanted to help him. And, like many teenagers, she assumed that she could not talk to her parents about what her boyfriend was saying. She assumed that she could handle something as heavy and important as a suicide threat by herself.

• • •

When you find your teenager in the midst of a miniature marriage, you must ask her if she is afraid to develop other friendships because she fears that her partner will kill himself. If this is the case, you should talk to her about the fact that she does not have the training or background to deal with suicidal thinking. She is, in fact, becoming the secondary victim of her partner's negative beliefs. A pattern you will often see in miniature marriages is that one partner is stable, holding things together, while the other partner is unstable.

As the parent, once you find out that your child is locked in an obsessive relationship with another teen, you need to alert all interested parties that large changes have to occur. I am an advocate of the parents of both teenagers getting together to discuss the situation with the teenagers present. The parents' job in such situations is to let the teenagers know that the "reset button" is about to be pushed, and life is going to return to normal. They will be allowed to talk on the telephone for no more than fifteen to twenty minutes at a time, and total phone contact will be limited to one hour per day. School nights will be reserved for academic pursuits. Both teenagers will be expected to become socially competent, in that they will each be expected to have other friends, to be engaged in school or sports-related activities, to have a real life. If either of the teens involved turns suicidal or shows strong indications of depression, it is to be handled by appropriate mental health professionals.

• • •

In one case I recently worked with, in which the boy was the stable partner in the miniature marriage and the girl was the unstable partner, the boy was actually relieved to tell his mother what was going on. He asked her to tell his girlfriend's mother that he could no longer be in the relationship. For months he had been dealing with her suicide threats and explosive behavior, and he did not know how to find his way out. His mother agreed to let her mother know how often the girl called, because at first she attempted to page him night and day and would phone relentlessly. The girl's parents were able to use the reports coming from the boy's mother to get treatment for her, as the reports helped them to realize the magnitude of the girl's insecurities and obsessive nature.

Hopefully, you will not have to go this far, if you find out early that your child is becoming involved in a miniature marriage. If you keep your own child busy with family activities, academics, sports, and maintaining friendships with long-term friends, she probably won't have time to get involved in a miniature marriage. You should talk with her openly about how such relationships are unrealistic because they suck up all available time and get in the way of the ongoing activities and friendships which she is already committed to.

In general, teenagers who are already busy and committed, but who get into miniature marriages, will quickly find the relationship overwhelming and beat a hasty retreat. It is important to talk to them about realizing when relationships are balanced and appropriate and when they are not. If your teen tells you that his relationship is more important than school and friends, be on the lookout for trouble and begin to set limits on phone time, dating, and so on.

Another indication of trouble is when you find your teenager, who might get ten dollars per week allowance and another twenty per week mowing lawns or washing cars, wanting to spend two hundred dollars on his girlfriend for her birthday. In general, your rule should be that your teenagers are not allowed to either give or accept expensive gifts. Such gifts serve to formalize and legitimize the miniature marriage and are the emotional equivalent of a wedding ring.

Some of the biggest questions about miniature marriages revolve around sex and birth control. If your teenager has been involved in a miniature marriage for three months or more, you should assume that he and his girlfriend are sexually active. And you should assume that they are having unprotected sex.

I know that debates rage about the issue of contraceptives. One camp holds that giving contraceptives to teenagers only encourages them to be sexually active. Another camp holds that they're going to have sex anyway, so giving them contraceptives decreases the risk of early pregnancy and does not really result in increased frequency of intercourse. My own position is pragmatic. I suggest that parents make birth control available to teenagers who are at high risk of being sexually active. Partners in a miniature marriage are certainly at high risk. I also let parents know that the setting that most teenagers use for being sexually active is their own bedroom. If your child is involved in a miniature marriage, you are foolish to leave her and her partner alone in your home. I've met far too many parents who, though home, allow their teenager and partner to head to the bedroom and close the door, ostensibly to "study" (anatomy, I suspect).

The other thing that I ask parents to do when their child is in a miniature marriage, but when the parent is forced to be out of the house most of the day or night due to work, is to either take personal leave time to make random visits to the house or have a trusted neighbor monitor the driveway and make random inspections inside.

A serious mistake that I see parents make is to treat the teenage boyfriend or girlfriend like a new husband or wife. While I don't mean to imply that parents should be rude or indifferent to their teenager's special friend, they should most certainly keep things in proportion. Some parents, for example, buy gifts for their daughter's boyfriend on his birthday or for Christmas. This will make him feel like a son-in-law. Likewise, I've known parents who allow their son's girlfriend to go on vacations with them or who can't go out to dinner as a family without the miniature partner in tow. All of this serves to solidify the relationship as a miniature marriage that has parental blessing.

The advice that I give to parents in such situations is to keep their teenager grounded in reality: "Sorry, this vacation is just for family." "No, Jamie may not come to dinner with us tonight. Tonight is for family only." Such advice serves, ultimately, to give guidance to parents on how to talk to their children about miniature marriages. I suggest that parents begin to talk to their children about miniature marriages long before their children begin to date. This is the same advice I give parents about drugs and about sex. Talk to your child about it well before it is likely to be an issue in her life. If you try to talk to her about it after the fact, your job becomes that much harder.

Here are examples of the replacement ideas parents should use in an attempt to make sure that their teenagers are thinking clearly about dating and relationships:

- Keep your relationship in perspective. While it is important to you, the most important issues for teenagers revolve around education, job training, and mastering the skills necessary to achieve the type of lifestyle that you envision for yourself.

- Evenings during the school week are primarily for studying and "feeding your brain," or for participating in school-sponsored activities. The weekend is for social activities and fun.

- Do not form relationships with people who need to be "fixed." Your job as a teenager is to study, to socialize, and to have fun. Trying to fix someone is a guaranteed way to make life feel like work instead of fun. If your boyfriend is suicidal or has serious mental health concerns, tell your parents so they can alert his parents to seek appropriate help.

- It is not possible for one person to meet all of your needs in life. If your girlfriend is pressuring you to give up your other friends and activities, be careful. She will continue to demand more and more of you, until you are miserable.

- If your relationships ends, it is not the end to happiness. Everyone experiences the loss of a relationship. Stay optimistic. You will find yourself attracted to many other people before you finally find your life partner.

- Do not build your relationships around your fears. Maintain a strong sense that you have something good to offer to others. If someone you are attracted to does not find you attractive in return, it does not mean that you are a failed individual. It only means that the two of you are not a good match.

Chapter 8

I Must Be Going Crazy

All of the Freudian notions about Id, Ego, and Superego and all of the Jungian notions about the dark side of the unconscious mind that mental health professionals encounter in their training seem to be interesting, but outdated ideas until you run into a child or teenager who tells you that there is a voice inside her head that is shouting for her to harm herself or others. If she tells you this voluntarily, which is unlikely, she may also admit that she feels like she has little control over the voice and that sooner or later it is going to make her do something really bad.

While it is relatively rare, there is a group of seemingly normal children or teens out there who, when placed under extremely high levels of pressure, have this experience. When this happens, all of the darker, hidden, unspoken urges of the human mind seem to coalesce into an angry, disembodied voice that seems to be going for a ride inside your own skull.

WHEN KIDS HEAR VOICES IT IS NOT ALWAYS THEIR IMAGINARY FRIEND

Experience has taught me to ask about this phenomenon when I work with children I know to be under huge stress. I explain to the child or teenager I'm talking to that some people have an experience that they keep secret from everyone because they don't want anyone to think that they are crazy. I tell them that for some people it feels like there is a voice in their head that is not really their own voice, a voice that they don't have any control over. The voice tells them to do frightening things or bad things, things that they know they should not do. The voice often claims that it can control them or has power over them, or that it can make them do things that they don't want to do. Most kids, thankfully, look at me like I'm the one who is crazy. Often times they will simply say, "No. What do you think, I'm crazy or something?" But every now and then, a child or teenager will look back at me, bolt upright and still, eyes wide, like she has just run into someone who can hear her thoughts without her permission.

What is this voice, anyway, and what can we do about it? I will be the first to admit that, from an academic viewpoint, it is interesting to spend time theorizing about the mental mechanisms underlying such an event, and it seems important to try to understand how and why such things happen. At the same time, practicality and expediency demand that we also quickly come up with a plan to protect children and adolescents who are experiencing this phenomenon.

While we talked earlier about the internal "voice" being the result of unconscious thoughts and urges filtering up into the conscious mind, there is really no way to measure, prove, or disprove such theoretical formulations. I have noticed, however, that most of the children and teenagers I have worked with who go through this phenomenon are caught up in a situation that they feel they have little control over, and they are angry and stressed because of it. From an interpretive standpoint, the angry voice that they hear in their own head is probably a representation of feelings of rage and anger so strong that the child cannot admit that he has them, so the mind is forced to express the negative feelings through other means. From a parenting standpoint, the appearance of a symptom so drastic as a disembodied voice is a clear signal that it is time for the parent to take over, because the child is, by any psychological standard, adrift.

The first step is to rapidly survey your child's or teenager's life in an attempt to find the sources of stress that are behind the feelings of helplessness and anger. With prepubescent children, stress may be due to feeling overwhelmed by school or may be due to being picked on or threatened by others. Often the real sources of stress are in the home. Maybe their parents are fighting and arguing too much. Sometimes they are being physically or sexually abused. For teenagers, the sources of stress can be the same as for children. In addition, stress can reach overwhelming levels when teens are caught up in bad dating or love relationships. It is the parents' obligation to hunt down the sources of stress in a child's or teenager's life and to take control.

The second step toward helping a child or teenager feel safe and contained in the face of such a drastic symptom is to immediately seek professional help. Your child will need to schedule a series of meetings with a mental health therapist who has experience in helping children through such high levels of stress. Your child will also need to see a child psychiatrist who is familiar with the phenomenon we are describing and who can prescribe medications to help control and decrease their perception of being stressed out.

Your third move is to give some careful consideration to just exactly how you or the therapist should talk to a child going through high levels of depression and stress. I've learned through experience that if your child or teenager strikes you as being extremely depressed or stressed out, you should go ahead and ask about the voice. You must be very straightforward, not hesitant or frightened. If you ask about the voice in a frightened way, it sends a message to the child that you don't want to send. You want to let your child or teenager know that he is safe and that you are in charge.

You can rest assured that if you do not ask children about hearing the internal voice, they will rarely tell. Children and adolescents seem to instinctively believe that there is something so peculiar about it, something so strange, that it must foreshadow something horrible. While children and teenagers are quick to hide this experience, once it is out they will tell you that going through it has made them feel miserable and frightened and that thoughts about their own sanity have dominated their minds.

Here are the ground rules for working with this experience: Unless you see clear indications of disintegration of ability to function, as in childhood schizophrenia, a rare (some would say mythical) condition in which a child's thought process is becoming increasingly disturbed and in total disarray, acknowledge to the child that you know for a fact that hearing the voice does not mean in any way, shape, or form that she is "crazy." Tell your child that the fact that she is hearing the voice has helped you to understand that she must be under a huge amount of stress and that she has been worrying too much.

One of the things that you or a therapist will need to talk to your child about is the fact that the voice cannot make him do anything. It is interesting and helpful for your child to talk about the things that the voice is telling him it can make him do, because this will tell you specifically what his fears revolve around. While the voice sometimes tells a teenager that it is going to make him harm himself or others, what it usually tells him to do is to act in an antisocial or shocking manner around others. The voice will typically urge him to do things like toss chairs through windows, turn over tables, yell or scream in public, and so on. The voice will claim that it can actually make him do such things. When it speaks, sometimes it whispers that it has control, and sometimes it shouts.

Another point that you or a therapist should talk to your child about is that he will feel like the voice is monstrous in size and strength. Some children and teenagers have described the voice to me as being as tall as a building, huge, gigantic. Invariably, they agree when I ask them if it feels like the voice is a monster.

I always indicate to children and teenagers that the voice is indeed a monster, but I am quick to say that it is a monster that is only two inches tall. My proof for this is that, invariably, while the child or teenager I am talking to has been almost paralyzed with fear that the voice is going to take control and make him do something bad, it has yet to happen.

In truth, most children and teenagers have been able to resist the voice's urgings for months before anyone found out what was going on. The child or teenager will tell me that, while he has been able to resist thus far, he is fearful that he will not be able to resist forever.

At this point I begin to give the child or teenager a visual metaphor to use in thinking about the monster. I explain again that, while it is a monster, it is only two inches tall. I ask the child to visualize the monster running around down on the floor, bellowing and roaring, shaking its tiny fists in the air and claiming to have enormous power. Then I ask the child to visualize taking his foot and squishing the monster like a bug.

"Squishing" the monster does not make it go away immediately. But it does give the child a sense of hope that he can challenge the voice and regain a sense of control. I have found that once the child or teenager begins an active mental battle with the voice, by telling it that it has no control or telling it to shut up and go away, the voice begins to change. At first the child will report that such challenges enrage it, and it shouts and screams that it does have control and that it is going to make him do something really bad. This can be a frightening time, and it becomes particularly important for the child to get visible, dramatic proof that the voice cannot make him act in an out-of-control manner.

ULTIMATE PROOF

I have a procedure that I have used in my office on a number of occasions. On paper it sounds quite dramatic. In reality it is really quite straightforward and simple. I explain to the child I am working with that it is now time to prove that the voice really has no control at all. This sometimes makes the child nervous, as you might reasonably expect, because of the fear associated with going through the experience of hearing the voice to begin with.

I acknowledge that fear, but I am quick to guarantee that the child will win. I then hand her a rock that I have on a shelf in my room, actually part of a geode that has been cut in half. I say that what I want her to do is to allow the voice to actually take control so that it can throw the rock through my picture window.

I am quick to explain that I do not want her to just pretend that the voice has control and throw the rock herself. I want her to allow the voice to literally take control of her body so that it is the voice, not the child, that is throwing the rock.

Suffice it to say that I have yet to replace my window. While this makes the child nervous at first, I invariably see a smile of relief come over her face when she realizes that, for all of the voice's whispering and shouting about its power, it is too small to lift the rock.

After such a session, I explain to my client that the voice will not be gone just yet. It may be quiet for a while, but it is likely to reappear and make claims such as "I didn't really want to make you throw the rock. I could have if I wanted to." I instruct my client to simply ignore this, because it has now been proven quite emphatically that the voice has no real power other than to bug her. I tell the child that because the voice has been proven to be powerless, somewhere in there, soon, it will begin to fade and eventually go away.

I understand that all of this sounds drastic, perhaps unbelievable. Children, teenagers, and adults who have been through the experience of the internal voice will understand, while those who have not been through it probably won't. It is my belief that as long as the child or teenager is taught not to worry too much about the voice, is not told that he is mentally ill, and is given the opportunity to challenge and confront the voice, it will eventually fade away. Sometimes the fading takes several months to be complete, sometimes only several weeks. In any case, it does go away.

Parents can help speed the process by taking control and eliminating external stressors. If your child's schedule is too full, this may mean pulling him out of activities, such as sports and clubs, for a while. Sometimes it means a couple of days off of school, with strict instructions not to study, but to just rest and relax during a long weekend. Sometimes it means telling your teenager that he may have to cool it with a stressful relationship.

In overview, here are some replacement beliefs you should explain to your child or teenager should you become aware that he is experiencing the internal voice. Teaching them how to think correctly about this experience is the key to resolving it quickly.

- Hearing the voice does not mean you are crazy, it only means you are stressed. It will go away in time as long as we do something about it.
- It is not possible for the internal voice to actually make you do anything. The only real power it has is to bug you. This will go away also.
- The voice does not have any religious significance. You are not being possessed by demons or Satan or spirits. While this experience is very uncomfortable, it is being caused by ordinary stress.

- Talking about all of the stresses in your life will help make you feel better. The more you keep what you are feeling secret, the worse you are likely to feel.
- When your stress level gets this high, you need to take a few days off. It is OK to take a few days off of school to get some rest. It is OK to decrease your other commitments, such as sports and clubs, until you feel better. Taking some time off will make you feel better.
- If a romantic relationship is causing this level of stress, it is best to consider decreasing the commitment to the relationship. Teenage relationships should be a source of enjoyment and fun, not a source of high stress

Chapter 9

My Parent's Didn't Love Me Enough

People who grew up in the absence of enough love or attention will often tell you that they feel hollow inside or that they have a big empty spot in the middle of their chest. I refer to this as the hole in the middle of the soul, a metaphor for what happens when children do not believe they receive sufficient nurturing.

Whether real or perceived, the reasons for not receiving enough love and attention are varied. Sometimes parents die. Sometimes parents work too many hours or have to travel as part of their job. Sometimes they drink too much, either passing out or becoming abusive.

Years back, when I used to work with depressed adults, one of the things that I noticed was that a startling number of them reported similar histories. Many of them came from families in which at least one of the parents was emotionally unavailable. Sometimes it was due to death. But to a large degree clients reported that their parents had been vertical, so to speak, throughout most of their childhood. They were very much alive, but emotionally unavailable for a variety of reasons.

AGE SIX AND AT THE CROSSROADS

Many of these depressed adults reported that by age six they were already having strong feelings about not being loved enough. Being children, their six-year-old thinking was egocentric. They believed, as most children do, that everything happens because of them. They assumed that if their mom or dad was not nice to them, it had to be because either they were bad children or they were not worthy of being loved.

Coming to the conclusion that they were bad children or unworthy children left them at a crossroads. They had two choices. They could learn quickly not to care what adults think, or they could try to become very good at something in order to get the unavailable parent's attention. Many of the depressed adults that I worked with reported that they set about the latter course of action, trying to be the best in their class at something.

This is how it would go: Our first grader, believing that he can gain the unavailable parent's love by doing something extraordinary, sets out to be the best reader. He works and pushes and when the grades come out, if he is successful, he takes them home for the parent to see. The parent, because she is emotionally unavailable, takes no notice.

Our child is now at another crossroads. He has done well by any reasonable standard. But, since he could not get the unavailable parent's approval and love, in his own mind he has failed to do enough. So, in addition to being the best reader, he pushes himself to become the best at penmanship. When the grades come out again, he takes them home, now being among the best at reading and at writing. Still, the unavailable parent fails to take notice, and our child's self-doubt begins to deepen.

You can see where this is headed. The child will try to get good at more and more things, hoping that his unavailable parent will finally notice and begin to pay genuine attention. This doesn't happen, sad to say. And, sooner or later, the child will crash and burn because the weight of trying to be so good at so many things in the absence of true parental attention and support is just too much.

When he crashes, he will enter a lengthy period of depression. He is unlikely to understand that he is depressed. While he knows clearly that he feels sad or tired all of the time or that he is dissatisfied with his life, he is unlikely to let others know. His peers and teachers, having watched him get good at so many things over the years, will continue to think of him as talented and bright. They will all be confused because he is not living up to his potential. They begin to wonder why his grades are slipping and where his motivation went. While he is aware that others see him as being capable, he is more aware of his own self-doubt.

Fast forward: The child is now an adult, sitting in my office. He doesn't feel very connected to anyone. Maybe he drinks too much. People less talented than he are getting ahead of him at work because he can't find the motivation to perform up to his abilities. He feels depressed.

At some point in the therapy, he will tell me that he has this big empty spot in the middle of his chest, right where his heart should be. His abiding sense of emptiness, I believe, is the reverberation of lost nurturing, the painful sense of what might have been, but wasn't.

• • •

As a parent, you can only recognize whether or not your child is at risk for developing this hole by confronting yourself about the environment he is being raised in. This is not an easy confrontation. One family I worked with a number of years ago had a father and a mother who were obviously nuts about each other. The father's work took him to Europe routinely for several weeks at a time. He was very well compensated for his travel, and his family lacked for nothing. But his family was also in total disarray. His wife was overwhelmed by the demands of having two sons with Attention

Deficit Hyperactivity Disorder. The oldest one, twelve at the time I knew them, was also highly defiant. He had been identified by his school system as eligible for talented and gifted education, but he could not be placed into the classes due to his poor grades. He used to blister his father in family meetings when we discussed his grades and his lack of motivation. "What do you care?" he'd ask. "You're never home anyway!"

. . .

I'm currently working with sisters, ages twelve and fourteen. The mother has left her husband because he stays drunk all of the time and is a yeller and a screamer. The girls say that their father did not hit them or abuse them in any way, although they did see him hit their mother on several occasions. Usually he was sleeping off a hangover.

The main thing the girls talk to me about is all of the arguing that went on between their parents. I ask them questions about how they feel about their mother leaving their father. Many sociologists tell us what a horrible event divorce is in a child's life. In this case the girls tell me they are happy about it. They have lost what little they had financially and live even more modestly than before. Yet they tell me they're happier than they were when their parents lived together.

. . .

These two cases are from opposite ends of the social spectrum. The people in the first case are rich and educated, and the ones in the second case are poor and work unenviable jobs to make ends meet. The children in the first case began to act out angrily because they didn't think their father spent enough time with them. The children in the second case are docile and have lowered their expectations of life to the point where they expect nothing. I wonder if either one of these viewpoints is healthy.

FILLING THE GAP

Preventing children from developing the hole in the middle of the soul requires that there be at least one engaged parent who is willing to take strong action to see that children do not grow up feeling ignored or unloved. What can parents do to make sure that their children do not end up with this hole? In an intact home, the parents must function as a unit. If the parents are continually at odds and always fighting, there is little chance for their children to have a stable platform from which to grow and develop healthfully. As I am forced to say to parents on occasion, "Bury the ax, or bury the child."

If a child is being raised in a situation in which one parent is indifferent or unavailable but the other parent is engaged, the engaged parent is placed in the uncomfortable position of letting the partner know that disengaged parenting will not be tolerated. Children have a strong natural drive to seek closeness, warmth, and nurturing. When it is refused them, it leads them to believe that there is something wrong with them, or that they have done something wrong, or that they are not worthwhile. These inevitable side effects of disengagement cannot be accepted.

Parents must refuse to sacrifice their children's emotional development for the sake of careers and habits. By careers, I mean the types of jobs which keep people, typically men, away from the home. While I understand that long hours and travel are sometimes part of a person's chosen profession, care has to be taken to mitigate the effect of travel and absences. I know one father, for example, who travels with a web camera that he can hook up to his computer. Even though he may be hundreds of miles away, he can still have a face-to-face conversation with his kids over the Internet. He is aware that this is a poor substitute for his physical presence, and he is thinking seriously about changing his career.

By habits, I mean a wide variety of activities. The obvious bad habits are alcohol and drugs. No child is capable of competing with alcohol and drugs, and parents cannot be involved with substances and children at the same time. There are other habits that can be just as damaging, however. Some parents spend all of their free time on the golf course, or working on cars, or painting pictures. These are wonderful activities to expose children to and to engage in with them. When children are held outside of such activities and not included, it has the same effect as if the parent is sitting in a room drunk. I know one teenager who tells me he secretly empties his father's booze down the drain. I know another teenager who tells me that she throws away her father's tennis balls.

There are often two situations that converge and can be quite explosive. Because of my book, *The Defiant Child*, I get many referrals and phone calls about children and teenagers who are ripping up the house. Many times the problem has already been properly diagnosed as Oppositional Defiant Disorder before I meet the children. But I find that there are a significant number of children and teenagers I see who, while defiant, are also being raised in a home situation with either a disengaged parent or a parent who has disappeared. The combination of emotionally unavailable parent and defiant behavior on the part of the child or teenager makes for a combustible mixture.

Parents of defiant children who are living in a household with an emotionally unavailable parent should not automatically assume that their child's anger and acting out are necessarily symptoms of Oppositional Defiant Disorder. It is equally likely, if not more likely, that the anger is due to feeling abandoned. It is important for parents to remember that before children and teenagers get to the point of being depressed enough to actually receive the medical diagnosis of depression, they often go through a stage of anger and rage because they feel ignored and unloved.

PUNISHMENT VERSUS LOVE

People often ask me what are appropriate punishments for defiant children. While I have spent lots of time thinking about this question and inventing various techniques, when I know that a child is depressed I ask the parents to use other methods first. My favorite method is to have the parents make sure that they increase the amount of physical contact they have with their child. I ask them to make sure that their younger children are getting plenty of lap time and that their teenagers are getting plenty of time leaned up against them on the couch while watching TV or talking. Depressed children and teenagers who are cranky and explosive often respond remarkably well to good firm back rubs and head scratches. Theoretically, the point would be that a depressed child is not easily capable of soothing himself. When the parent steps in and provides heavy physical nurturing, it is like balm to the hole in the middle of the soul.

We have to be exceptionally clear with depressed children and teenagers about how they should think about their disengaged, emotionally unavailable parents. Remember, depressed children and teenagers have a tendency to almost automatically believe negative things about themselves. In the midst of their self-criticism, they can fail to understand the effect that lost nurturing may have had on how they feel, function, and think about themselves. Here are some things to discuss with your teenager if you believe that he has been negatively affected by a disengaged parent:

- You are not the cause of your parent's disengagement. While it is true that certain children can place a real wedge between themselves and their parents with their antisocial behavior, depressed children are rarely the types to be the cause of parental disengagement. Chances are that your parent's distance comes from her own personality style.

- You cannot afford to take your parent's distancing and lack of emotional availability personally. It is difficult not to take it personally when you do not feel love flowing in your direction. But the minute you take it personally, you will begin to believe it is your fault.
- While it would be wonderful to get the kind of love a parent gives a child, it may be too late. Your only answer is to learn to like and respect yourself. This means being clearheaded and realistic about how you judge yourself, rejecting the natural tendency toward self-criticism that comes with lost nurturing.
- Don't make the mistake of looking for a boyfriend or girlfriend who can make up for the lost nurturing. This puts your partner in the position of treating you like a child and acting like a parent to you. While such relationships do exist, they are totally unbalanced and not fun.
- Even though you were raised by an emotionally unavailable parent, you should avoid coming to the conclusion that life holds nothing good, fun, or interesting. The world holds many interesting possibilities. Let your engaged, involved parent lead you into the fun that is there.
- Avoid expecting only the minimum in life, which is the natural outcome of lost nurturing. Avoid becoming involved in relationships that offer only the minimum. You are not lucky because your partner does not abuse substances, run around, or hit you. That is the least you should demand.

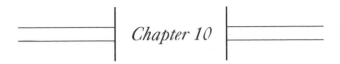

Chapter 10

Substances Will Make Me Happy

All of the teenagers I work with tell me that by the time they reach high school, they have had some contact with illegal drugs. This is not a misprint. *All.*

Here is how I arrived at this statistic: I ask everyone I work with who is of high school age if they have either used drugs or alcohol themselves or if they have friends or acquaintances their age who they know for sure use drugs or alcohol. Combine these two categories, and they add up to everybody.

There's even worse news. The picture I painted above is actually somewhat rosy. In truth, there are far too many sixth, seventh, and eighth graders who know almost as much about drugs as their high school counterparts.

Most teenagers tell me that by the time they begin to drive, there is nowhere they go that drugs and alcohol are not available should they decide to use them. This includes parties, the mall, school and athletic events, camp, rehab centers, detention facilities, and even church. The invasion of drugs into the teenage world is complete in ways that we never dreamed of.

• • •

There are several reasons for bringing up the issue of substances in a book that is about childhood depression. For one, substances cause teenagers to become depressed. Second, teenagers who are already depressed often turn to substances looking for relief. Teenagers who become depressed due to their substance use mistakenly continue to use out of a misguided hope that substances will eventually make them feel better. Substances also bring teenagers into contact with people they would be better off not having contact with, people who will often prove to be harmful to them.

The point of all of this is that teenagers do not tend to believe that substances cause depression. Teenagers tend to believe, instead, that substances cause coolness. Along with coolness comes the illusion of maturity and power and radical rejection of the expectations of the adult world.

Teenagers who delve deeply into the illusory world created by substances tend to think a certain way. The following list, while not at all inclusive, gives a good overview of their beliefs:

- Having fun is more important than anything else, especially school.
- The main way to have fun is to "party." "Partying" involves using alcohol or drugs.
- Without substances, there can be no fun.
- The purpose of drinking alcohol is to get as drunk as physiologically possible. The more drunk you are, the more fun you are having.
- The purpose of using drugs is to get as wasted as possible. The more wasted you are, the more fun you are having.
- You depend upon your friends to explain to you just how much fun you had, since you are unlikely to remember. If you threw up or did something truly outrageous, then you must have been having maximum fun.

- It is desirable to be known as a rebel. The fastest and most convenient way to define yourself as a rebel is substance use.
- People who do not use substances are boring. Another term for people who do not use substances is "goody goody."
- Using substances proves that I am no longer a little kid.
- It is not my parents' business if I use substances. I get to make my own choices.
- My parents cannot tell me who my friends should be. I get to make my own choices.
- I am closer to my friends than I am to my own family.

Once they become depressed, the thinking of substance users becomes more blunted and pessimistic. They tend to think like this:

- I wish I knew how to have fun.
- Maybe if I party more, I will begin to have fun.
- I don't care what my parents think or what anybody else thinks about me.
- If I get wasted, maybe I can forget what I feel like inside.
- Nothing is really very likely to change anyway.

You don't have to look at these hopeless beliefs very long to realize what kinds of behaviors emanate from them. A pattern I see over and over in my office is one in which a teenager was doing quite well in his life right up to age fifteen, at which point the parents begin to suspect that aliens have come down, kidnapped their child, and replaced him with an evil clone. The way it happens is that in the year preceding turning fifteen, most teenagers begin to suspect that there are alternative ways to view the world than how Mom and Dad see things. At about this same time, they run into peers who have already made the leap into alternative thinking, who act as role models and guides for others who want to reject the adult world.

THE GIRL IN THE BLUE BANDANNA

Shelby is a young woman I am working with at present who fits this process of rebellion and rejection of the adult world through substance use. The main thing she knows is that she does not want to be like her mother or father, both of whom are smart, perfectly nice individuals who would make good neighbors and friends for most of us. Shelby is among that very confused group of suburban teenagers who have grown bored and dissatisfied with their lives and who apparently believe that the true meaning of life has been revealed to street gangs from the Compton, California, ghetto. With breathtaking speed, she transformed from high-functioning, academically talented cheerleader and soccer player to gangster-rapping, bandanna-wearing, ghetto-talking, drug-using punk. She lectures me on how the world will kill you if you are not "down with a gang." She explains that she is protected because she has her "grrrlz" to hang with and to "take her back (guard her from attack from the rear by other gang grrrlz)." Currently she tends to run away from home for several days at a time about once a month. When she leaves, she hangs out with gangs and spends most of her day getting high and "chillin'" with small-time drug dealers.

I worry about Shelby. She is uncommonly bright, but as naive as she is smart. For her, her affiliations with her peers who see the world the way she sees it are the most important part of her life. She doesn't think about her family and doesn't think about her future. She has picked up that fatalistic belief that she will be dead by the time she is twenty-one, a belief of gang members who, unlike our young poser, are the real deal.

I'm in the midst of having talks with Shelby about the reality of the drug and gang-oriented world that she finds so fascinating, but thinks about in such romantic, misguided terms. I asked her a few days ago how many old drug dealers she had met. She told me none. I asked her why that would be the case, as it is quite easy to find middle-aged businessmen, lawyers, doctors, or teachers. She got the point, admitting that most of the street dealers that she would be likely to encounter were either dead or in jail before they got to middle age.

She insists that the world she is so fascinated with, the drug-oriented street gangs, is the "real world." I have to admit to her that there is certainly something real about it, because it does obviously exist. But I ask her if the street life is so great, why does the founder of gangster rap, the musician who calls himself Dr. Dre, live in a gated Tudor mansion in the suburbs? She does not like questions like this because they mess with her beliefs, her mental program.

If you have a teenager who has verged off into the party-oriented or drug-oriented or gang-oriented life, you have to be careful about how you talk to her so that you do not run her away. Part of what is so difficult about dealing with these teenagers is that they believe that their lifestyle is a legitimate alternative to your own, and they believe that their thoughts about the world are totally clear and realistic.

DEALING WITH KIDS IN THE DRUG ZONE

What should you do if you find out your teenager is deeply involved in substance use? Your first impulse will be to tell him that he is not allowed to see the people he is using with. Your next impulse will be to tell him that he can't leave the house until he is twenty-five. There is a lot to consider about each of these issues.

Your first task is to try to determine just how far your teenager has delved into substance use. Frankly, there is no accurate way to do this. You should certainly ask your teenager, just to see what he says, and you should balance this against what else you know about how he is living. If he is being academically successful, hangs out with generally good peers, and limits his use to relatively safe situations, you probably don't have to hit the panic button. While there is no way for parents of high school students to get comfortable with the idea of their kids trying drugs, a realistic appraisal would indicate that there is a high probability of it happening. You most certainly do have to talk to your teenager if this happens and make sure he is well educated about drugs. You have to make sure that he is not using drugs in an attempt to escape reality or to self-medicate. Again, as long as he is doing well in most phases of his life, this is probably not the case. His experimentation probably comes under the heading of life events that can be termed "painfully normal."

This does not mean, in any sense, that substance use should be tolerated. I have for years been an advocate of the following procedure: Once you find out that your child is using drugs, it is important to contact the parents of his friends to alert them to the fact that substances have invaded their peer group. Ask for a meeting at your house that all of the parents and all of the teenagers involved have to attend. Let them know that their drug use must stop, and in order to assure this, random drug screening tests will be administered at their respective doctors' offices. The parents can agree to share the outcomes of these tests. Let the teenagers know that all of the parents will be watching all of the teenagers closely. The parents will have the right to ask any of the teenagers to empty their pockets, take their car keys, search their cars, smell their breath, check their eyes, check their balance, and so on, if drug use is suspected. The parents should agree to keep in touch by telephone. Each teenager should be told that if his drug tests are positive, he will lose all driving privileges and all privileges of going anywhere with his friends until his parents can be safely sure that he is no longer using and does not pose a hazard to his friends and to the public at large.

But suppose you encounter a more serious situation. Your child is failing in school, hanging out with a peer group that is headed nowhere, and is probably driving your car around while he is using. Let us assume, also, that he is using substances in an attempt to make himself feel better or to escape the pressures of the real world. This is when you do hit the panic button. You will need to move in two directions in such a case. First, if your teenager is using substances and is depressed, chances are he is using in an attempt to make himself feel better. If he is not in counseling with a knowledgeable substance abuse therapist, get him into treatment. You will also need to consult with a child or adolescent psychiatrist regarding the use of antidepressant medications and/or brief hospitalization in order to make sure that your teen is receiving treatment at the necessary level of intensity.

Your second move is to disrupt his relationship with his peer group. While I do not see this as being necessary in situations like the first case I described above, it strikes me as absolutely necessary in situations in which your teenager is out of control and depressed to boot. There is little to be gained by allowing your teenager to continue to associate with peers who are leading him straight toward oblivion.

How do you disrupt these relationships? A technique I have had parents use in the past, when you know the names or addresses or phone numbers of the people who either supply your child with drugs or provide a place for him to use them, is to tell them that you will report them to the police if they continue to have contact with your child. Your strategy here is to make your child a liability to them, someone no longer worth hanging around. This technique is guaranteed to make your teenager angry. But what is the potential cost of not intervening strongly?

Another issue you are bound to encounter with the teenager who is using drugs is the fact that he is probably hiding them in your home. There is no reason to invade the privacy of a high-functioning, competent child or teenager. However, once you begin to suspect drug use, privacy is a moot point. Let your child or teenager know that you will be searching systematically, as well as requiring random drug screenings, until you are satisfied that substance use is no longer an issue.

There are a number of replacement beliefs that I try to get teenagers to accept about drugs and alcohol and lifestyle. Remember that it is not particularly easy to reprogram how teenagers think about drugs and alcohol if you wait until after the fact. By the time we make the attempt at reprogramming their thinking, many of them are already physically or emotionally addicted to substances and substance-oriented lifestyles. Many teenagers will be highly defensive about their habits and will attempt to protect their habits when they talk to you. It is best to start these discussions very early in life. These replacement beliefs can make for interesting discussions:

- Regarding being "radical": Being radical is actually quite desirable. Vincent van Gogh, Henry Ford, Harriet Tubman, Albert Einstein, Thomas Edison, Amelia Earhart, Martin Luther King. Do these names ring a bell? All of them went against conventional wisdom. All of them, in their day, were radical. It is simpleminded and mistaken to believe that you can become radical in any meaningful way by turning to drugs and alcohol, tough street attitude, public cursing, playing your music so loud that the people in the car in front of you can't hear the music in their own car, and so on. All of these things are easy to do. It is easy to get drunk or high, easy to act like a barbarian, easy to speak in profanities in family restaurants, and especially easy to twist the volume knob on your car stereo. Being truly radical involves stretching your intellect and creativity and motivation, all of which are easily wrecked by drugs.

- Substances turn everyone who comes into contact with them into liars. This goes along with the rather dark joke in the drug and alcohol rehab field. Question: How do you know when an alcoholic is lying? Answer: His lips are moving. Teenagers who are using substances will lie to all of their loved ones about the scope of their use. They will lie about who gave them the drugs or alcohol, or who sold it to them. They will lie about who they are hanging out with and about how much and how often their friends use. They fail to understand that they are lying and see this lying as loyalty.

- Nobody dreams at age five of growing up to be dependent on alcohol or drugs. The companies which make cigarettes and beer base their survival upon you coming to believe that their products are the gateway to fun and relaxation and stress reduction. In order to assure their own survival, these companies have spent billions of dollars on advertising in an attempt to get you to believe that their products are desirable. This is a form of mind control.

- Drugs are bigger and tougher than all of us. No one dreams of becoming an addict, yet millions of people do. If people can stop any time they want to, as most substance users claim, why do we have any addicts at all?

- Substances "whisper" to you to come back when you try to leave them. You'll think about them everywhere you go and will dream about them in your sleep. This tells you just how addicted you are.

- They don't call it dope for nothing. Virtually every teenager who gets heavily into street drugs suffers a large drop in academic and intellectual performance. Drugs make you stupid. If you doubt this, listen to your friends talk when you are straight and they are high.

Chapter 11

Nothing Will Ever Change

One of the saddest aspects of depression is loss of hope, the sense that nothing will ever change. Not all depressed people go through this. The ones who do are probably much more seriously depressed than the ones who don't. Think of it this way: If you are depressed, but hopeful that things might eventually change, you have at least some small amount of room left in your life for enjoyment. If you have no hope, you wake up each morning feeling like you have an elephant standing on your chest, an elephant that has no intention of moving.

Loss of hope is associated with much more than just lack of enjoyment. I suspect that loss of hope is a central factor in every case of suicide. Again, think of it this way: If you thought your life might get better, would you really try to kill yourself? Loss of hope is also central to many of the depressive beliefs we have talked about thus far, from "No one will ever like me" to "Death is an option." One way to help a person rid himself of depression is to try to restore his sense of hope.

WHERE DOES HOPE GO?

Loss of hope occurs for a number of different reasons. If a child or teenager is continually picked on or told bad things about himself by his parents or peers, his sense of hope for a bright future can diminish. A string of academic failures can make hope and optimism go away. Children and teenagers who live in families that argue or fight constantly, whether or not the fighting is fueled by substance use, become numb.

Numbness is actually an effective defense for what is going on around you. The problem with numbness as a defense is that it works too well. You may no longer feel pain, but you also no longer feel pleasure. Hope goes away when you do not feel pleasure, reminding us that hope and pleasure and happiness are all in delicate balance with each other.

In chapter 1 we talked about the linebacker and the girl who had to be hospitalized because her trust in adults was so drastically taken advantage of. When they entered counseling, both of these individuals had a strong sense that they would never feel better. They were resigned to feeling depressed forever, resigned to never enjoying anything, and resigned to lives that were bound to turn out badly. This type of resignation provides a good working definition of hopelessness.

Childhood hopelessness can lead to an adult life also marked by hopelessness, assuming the hopeless child or teenager does not kill herself somewhere along the line. This is one of the most important reasons to understand just how it is that hopeless children think and feel. In general, hopeless children and teenagers have hopeless beliefs in three particular areas of their lives: their future, their self-worth and abilities, and the people they live with or are forced to deal with frequently. Should we, for example, be surprised that hopelessness poisons the future? This is how hopeless children and teenagers think about the future:

- I won't live very long.
- I'll never be happy or have fun.
- There won't be anything good about my future.
- I have no ability to influence what will happen to me in the future.

Likewise, children and teenagers have a particular way of thinking about themselves and their abilities. For example:

- No one will ever love me or find me interesting.
- I'll never amount to anything.
- I can't influence the way I feel or think.

They particularly do not believe that their world, which they view as hostile, will ever be open to modification:

- My parents will never stop arguing and fighting.
- My parents will never stop drinking.
- The people in the neighborhood or at school who make me feel bad about myself will never change.
- The world will always be a bad place.
- No one will ever be nice to me.

In order to help a child or adolescent escape her sense of hopelessness, we have to interact with her on several different planes. First, we have to convince her that her sense of hopelessness is her depression whispering to her, fooling her into believing negative things. We have to tell her that we know that she desperately wants to escape the hopelessness she is feeling, but that she is not likely to escape until she takes a closer look at how she is thinking and what she believes. She will have to learn to distrust her thoughts and will have to learn to replace her hopeless beliefs with ideas that are more realistic and healthy.

She will, of course, tell you that it will not do any good to try to change anything, because she is doomed to feel the way she does. You will have to point out to her at that very moment that her depression is doing the talking and that these ideas are guaranteed to keep her depressed.

Take, for example, the issue of the future. We have to convince hopeless children and teenagers that no one has a crystal ball. Or, failing that, that the people who really do have crystal balls don't seem to know how to turn the things on to use them. None of us knows what the future holds. A conversation in which I use the ideas of double standards and proof might go this way:

TEEN: "I'm never going to feel happy. I just know that's how it's going to be."

ME: "How can you be sure? That is a pretty big conclusion to come to."

TEEN: "I just know, that's all."

ME: "Suppose I said that same thing to you. Suppose I said that I know for a fact that I will never be happy, not for the whole, entire, rest of my life. What would you think if you heard me say such a thing?"

TEEN: "I don't know."

ME: "Remember, I don't ever accept 'I don't know' as an answer to an important question, particularly when I know I'm talking to a smart person. What would you think?"

TEEN: "I'd think maybe you really think you would never be happy."

ME: "I might *think* that. But could I really *know* for a fact that I'd never be happy?"

TEEN: "No. You couldn't really know that."

ME: "Then how could you know what is going to happen in the future if I can't? Are you trying to tell me that you have some sort of special powers or something?"

TEEN: "No. It's not that I can really know it. It's just what I think."

ME: "Do you understand the difference between really knowing something to be a fact and just believing something? Like years ago, everybody *knew* that the world was flat and that you would fall off the edge of it if you went too far out in the ocean. It obviously wasn't true, but they treated it like it was. You can't *know* what you'll be doing next week, much less how you'll be feeling in one year. You've got to be careful about how you think."

TEEN: "Why?"

ME: "Because if you go around all day thinking that your life is bound to be unhappy, how will you end up feeling by the end of the day?"

TEEN: "Pretty bad."

ME: "Isn't that what you're doing to yourself already?"

We will have to also talk to her about what she is secretly thinking about herself, because this is where her sense of hopelessness is really coming from. If she felt good about herself, she would be able to see a future for herself. I'll continue to use the double standard and the idea of proof in talking to her:

ME: "You've been thinking like that for a long time, I bet. Thinking that you will never be happy."

TEEN: "Yes."

ME: "Suppose you knew that I thought the same way. What do I secretly think about myself, way down inside?"

TEEN: "I don't know. Really, I don't."

ME: "I understand. It's complicated. Think about it like this: Do you really think that it is possible for someone to like herself and at the same time believe that she will never be happy?"

TEEN: "Probably not."

ME: "Then what does that tell me about you?"

TEEN: "That I probably don't like myself."

ME: "I want to hear more about what you really do think about yourself."

At this point, I will insist that she give me real proof about her shortcomings. When we find things that she really does need to change about herself, we will make a plan for doing so. When we find negative things that she believes about herself in the absence of any real proof, I will insist that she replace her negative thinking, her hopeless beliefs, with more realistic thinking about herself. You can use this technique with any of the hopeless beliefs.

RESTORING HOPE

We have to help a hopeless child understand that the world can seem like a fun place again. Making the world seem like fun again is not an easy task when the hopeless child tells you that she does not enjoy doing anything. At the same time, unless she gets out and does activities that most other people consider to be fun, she is unlikely to ever report that she has had any fun. The logic goes like this: If I personally have not had any fun, that means the world is not a fun place.

I've listened to arguments like this so many times in the past that I finally came up with the concept of "forced fun." I know that it sounds like a contradiction in terms. The way it works, though, is to explain to the depressed, hopeless individual that she is not likely to ever feel good unless she goes out and does the things that she used to enjoy or does things that people in general enjoy. I warn her not to come back and tell me that the first time she went out with her friends for a pizza was not fun. I explain that depression and hopelessness rob people of the ability to experience pleasure. In order to ever have fun again she will have to "kick start" fun the same way you have to kick start a small motorcycle. It might not work the first time. You have to be willing to do it over and over and over until it works. Go out with your friends for a pizza, or a movie, or to a park, or whatever, ten times before you come to any conclusions.

Some people will tell me that even after doing something with friends ten times, they still do not feel pleasure. A technique I use with people this stuck is to talk about their inability to experience the enjoyment of small things, to enjoy the moment. Once I am sure that they understand the concept of enjoying the moment, I ask them to go to their favorite ice cream shop, order the largest, most delicious, most elaborate ice cream dish they can think of, and sit there and see if they can truly feel angry at the world the whole time they are eating it.

Most people get my point, it being that you have to purpose-fully set out to find what is enjoyable in order to escape depression. You cannot wait passively for enjoyment and hope to come to you. You cannot wish that something or someone will rescue you from depression. While I do not wish to be overly simplistic, people trapped in a hopeless viewpoint must make some attempt to pull themselves out of depression by their own bootstraps. People who tell themselves that they cannot experience pleasure will be un-likely to experience it in anything. They must understand that they have programmed themselves to think that enjoyment is im-possible. Because they think this way, their prediction will always come true.

We must also be willing to listen with the fascinated ear to what depressed and hopeless children and teenagers tell us about their world. Let's return to how these individuals tend to think about other people in their lives who are making them unhappy or having a negative impact on them.

In talking with the hopeless child about the people she is hav-ing trouble with at school, we often will have to admit to her that yes, it is true, some of these people are unlikely to change. We cannot control how these individuals act. We can only control what we end up believing about ourselves after having interactions with skunks. As we discussed earlier, it is good to tell a hopeless child about how the human skunks of the world think and behave and to explain how they are trying to get her to feel bad about herself. We may need to remind her over and over that if she ends up feeling bad about herself because of what some skunk has said, then the skunk has won the game.

As parents, what do we do once we realize that we are the skunks, that we are the ones who are influencing our child to view the world in hopeless terms? The first step is to develop the willingness to even ask such a question. I have all too often had parents bring a child to see me because the child is depressed, only to have the parent get upset when I began to ask about the interaction between parent and child. The point would be to recall what we already know about structure. If you are raising a child in an unstable environment, if you are continually critical, if you are abusive physically, emotionally, or sexually, you are programming your child to believe negative ideas about the nature of her own life and the nature of the world around her. You have no right to ask your child or teenager to be hopeful until you are willing to challenge yourself to change how you behave toward her.

Once it becomes apparent to you that your child or teenager is caught up in a private sense of hopelessness, you have to take time to be alone with her and to talk to her at a philosophical level about the future. The goal of these talks is to help your child become optimistic. Keep in mind that depression has probably robbed her of whatever optimism she had. Optimism, from my perspective, is one of the most important cognitive and psychological characteristics that we can nurture in our children. Without it, it is difficult not to become depressed.

This is heady stuff, not necessarily easy to get into. These talks are made much more enjoyable over a pizza or an ice cream cone, because this in itself helps to demonstrate that life can be fun. These are some of the replacements for the hopeless beliefs that are causing your child to be depressed:

- Regarding "I won't live very long": If you are a gang member or hang out with gangs, this may very well be true. It may be best to begin to think about how you can go about getting out of your gang. If your gang is of the sort to put out an SOS (shoot on sight) on people who leave, you have all the more reason to leave. Talk to your parents or to an adult you can trust about your safety concerns.

- If you are not in a gang but are concerned about how long you will live: Depression often fools people into thinking that they are bound to have a short life. Your fears about how long you will live will go away once you feel better. The truth of it is, no one knows how long they will live. You might as well make the most of the time you have.

- If you wait passively for happiness, success, fun, or closeness with others to just "happen" to you, it probably won't happen. It is better to plan what you want for the future and go after it.

- You have many ways to influence your future. Among them are getting a good education, learning to work well in group settings, learning job skills that will be in demand in the future economy, making sure that your social skills are up to par, and making yourself an enjoyable individual to be around.

- Regarding "No one will ever like me": If you think like that, it may come true. Individuals who believe they will be rejected have a way of acting rejectable. If you are doing this, then of course others will avoid you. You will be much more attractive to the person you hope will find you desirable if you are emotionally secure and interesting to be around. This means confronting your own negative ideas about yourself, getting rid of the ones that have no basis in reality, and making a plan to fix your true shortcomings. While you are at it, reject the strategy of getting others to love you because they feel sorry for you. Pity is not the type of attention you need.

- Regarding "I can't help the way I feel or think": Yes you can. You must learn to think of your thoughts as being a program that is running in your mental computer. When you hear yourself think about your long-term beliefs (for example, your private thoughts about how you look, how smart you are, what others think about you), you are actually listening to your own program. If you hear a line of code in your program that is unusually negative (no one will ever love me, for example), it is your job to stop your mental computer, pull out that line of code, and examine it to see if it is based in reality. Faulty lines of code must be replaced with more realistic beliefs.

- Regarding the people in your life who are making you unhappy: You're right, they may never change. Can you afford to let such individuals be the ones who determine how you feel about yourself?

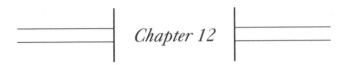

Chapter 12

Building a Treatment Strategy

Given that you have begun to educate yourself on what it feels and sounds like inside the head of a depressed child or adolescent, it is not likely now that you will encounter depressive symptoms in your child, such as loss of enjoyment, or crankiness, or a desire to sleep all day, and not have some idea about what might be behind it. You know now to ask yourself if it is being caused by biological forces, by stressors external to your child, or by the way your child thinks. You should now be ready to generate specific hypotheses about why your child may feel depressed.

For example, assume that your child is depressed and voices hopeless thoughts about his future. You will be right to worry about this. Your worrying will be much more productive if you begin to think about all of the potential reasons why your child has come to feel hopeless. It might be related to how the other children at his school are treating him. Maybe he has come to believe that he is not as good as they are or that he will never amount to much. It could be that, from his perspective, there is too much conflict at home and he thinks things will never change. It could be that he thinks he has to be perfect, and the fact that he can't be has left him dreading a lifetime of mistakes. Maybe he thinks he looks funny or thinks that others think he looks funny. These are all things for you to consider. Once you begin to put your finger on the cause of your child's distress, whether it is because of how he thinks, whether it is because of outside factors, or whether it is biochemical in nature, you can begin to plan what to do next instead of sitting passively by.

There are a number of steps that you may wish to take next. Thus far, you have learned primarily about the cognitive, thought-based causes for depression. You have learned how to talk to your child about what he is thinking and how to help him replace his depression-causing thoughts with more productive ways of thinking. Using this knowledge base to begin an ongoing dialogue with your child about what he is thinking and experiencing is absolutely the best thing you can do to help him escape depression.

I say that it is necessary for you to be deeply engaged with your child in talking not because I distrust the professional psychology and medical community to help in healing your child. I say this because any professional you see is likely to spend no more than an hour or two with your child each week, while you will be around him many times as much. Your understanding of how depressed children and teenagers think and view the world will give you a lot to talk about each day.

SEEKING PROFESSIONAL HELP

Should you seek the help of professionals? You should, most definitely. I believe that the first person to consult should be your pediatrician or family practitioner. Pediatricians and family practitioners are among the most broadly trained individuals in the medical field. They have the background and education to recognize the symptoms of depression. One of the things that I admire about the pediatricians and family practitioners I know is that they have a fierce loyalty to their patients and do not make referrals to mental health practitioners without knowing the quality of the practitioner's work. You should ask your doctor who she would want her own child to see for medication and counseling.

The phone company will probably not be pleased with me for suggesting that you pay no attention to yellow page ads. Choosing a therapist for your child by turning to the yellow pages is akin to throwing a dart. You never know what you are going to get. It might be tempting to go to the place that has the largest ad, the largest staff, the longest list of mental health concerns that are treated in their facility. The fact is that the ad can tell you nothing of their true expertise. It only tells you how much money the group spends on advertising.

You also want to be suspicious of calling telephone numbers for referral services in your area. Most referral services are in the business of giving you names of practitioners who have paid to have their names listed. The person who answers the telephone and gives you names of people or offices to call is simply reading a list. At their most high tech, referral services will ask you where you live and generate a list of names for you based on whose office is within a half-hour drive of your house. This is something less than the mark of quality you should be seeking in health care purchasing decisions.

You should also be careful when asking your insurance carrier to recommend mental health practitioners in your area. Mental health providers, myself included, contract with numerous insurance carriers to be what is known as a "preferred provider." This means that a practitioner has agreed to discount charges to the insurance company by around twenty-five percent, in return for being included on the insurance company's list of providers that is given to every policyholder. Being listed as a provider can make or break a practice financially in some markets. But being listed says nothing about the quality of a provider's work.

Like some physicians, some mental health practitioners associated with health maintenance organizations sign what is known as a capitation agreement with the insurance carrier. The insurance company pays the practitioner a set amount of money each month to provide care for each of its insureds. If the cost of all of the treatment actually provided by the practitioner that month is less than the amount paid by the insurance company, the doctor gets to pocket the difference. If the cost exceeds the amount paid by the insurance company, the doctor loses money. From the insurance company's perspective, this gives practitioners an incentive to be careful about how many tests to order for patients, how many patients to refer to specialists, and so on. From my perspective, this is a bribe and an unethical arrangement for medical and mental health professionals to be part of. You need to know if any of the practitioners you employ in your child's treatment is involved in capitation agreements with insurance companies. This does not mean that your practitioner is not excellent, but it does mean that the financial agreement with the insurance company may affect your child's treatment without your knowledge. You need to know the details.

My general advice is that you telephone the practitioner's office and ask to set up a brief face-to-face interview to get a sense of what working with her would be like. In particular, ask about her expertise in the field of children and adolescent mental health. My personal tendency is to avoid referring to practitioners who do not have heavy experience in working with children and adolescents or who do not spend a majority of their day doing so. I frankly distrust generalists to have a grasp of the subtlety of the issues presented by children, adolescents, and their families. If a practitioner is going to specialize in child and adolescent mental health, he should do so. Likewise, he should specialize in adults if that is his interest. It is unlikely that anyone can do both at the highest level. You should be warned that many of the largest insurance companies seek out large group practices of mental health "generalists" to provide services for them, seeing specialists as too narrowly focused.

MENTAL HEALTH PRACTITIONERS

Within the mental health field, the two major types of practitioners are medical and psychological. Medical practitioners are primarily psychiatrists, individuals who attend medical school and who then go on for specialized internship and residency training in mental health. They usually hold an M.D. or a D.O. degree. While many psychiatrists are generalists, there are others who specialize in child and adolescent psychiatry. Those who are board certified in child psychiatry have passed a series of exams and have obtained a level of training that is generally recognized as the highest in their specialty area. Psychiatrists are the only mental health practitioners licensed to prescribe medication.

Psychiatrists traditionally receive extensive training in diagnosing serious mental disorders. In the past psychiatrists were trained to provide counseling and psychotherapy, but pharmaceutical interventions have required most of their attention in recent years. In general, most psychiatrists confine their office and hospital practices to diagnosing mental health disorders and treating them with medication.

The psychological practitioners are made of up psychologists, licensed professional counselors, clinical social workers, and, to a smaller extent, registered nurses and nurse practitioners. Psychologists typically hold a doctoral degree (Ph.D., Ed.D., Psy.D., D.Sc.), although some states allow psychologists to practice with a masters degree. Psychologists attend graduate school and are typically trained in a wide variety of psychotherapy techniques, from analytic to behavioral to cognitive psychology. Additionally, psychologists are the only mental health professionals with training in administering and interpreting psychological tests.

Licensed professional counselors hold either a doctoral degree or a masters degree in counseling. Clinical social workers typically hold the Masters in Social Work (MSW) degree. Some do go on to obtain doctoral degrees, although most of these individuals go into academic careers. Professional counselors and social workers receive extensive training in family and individual psychotherapy.

It is interesting to think about the similarities and differences in the practitioners who make up the mental health field. A natural question would be which group of providers is the best. The answer is that no group of practitioners has distinguished itself by being better than the others. You will find that while the mental health professions look like they are in competition with each other, each group has different training, which gives them the ability to approach an issue from a different perspective. Psychiatrists are invaluable in treating cases of severe depression because they have expertise in medication. At the same time, this profession has drawn considerable fire for the dependence on treating with medication alone and the tendency to have patients take too many medications at once. To add to the difficulty, child psychiatrists are as scarce as the proverbial hen's teeth in most areas of the country, and it sometimes takes many weeks, if not months, to get an appointment with one.

The psychological practitioners are invaluable for their grasp of behavioral psychology, family dynamics, and personality theory. Psychologists tend to receive lengthy course work and training in how to formulate behavior change plans. With their expertise in testing, they can sometimes get to the subtle issues underlying psychological problems quite rapidly. Other mental health practitioners often refer their patients to psychologists for testing in an attempt to make the treatment process move along more quickly and more accurately.

Psychologists and licensed professional counselors have traditionally been trained in the methods of depth psychotherapy, the attempt to get at the underlying cause of a problem as opposed to simply treating its symptoms. The criticism about individual psychotherapy is that it tends to take a long time to be effective and can become quite expensive.

Clinical social workers have traditionally been the experts in family therapy and in treating the effect that family has on the individual. Many do choose to work with individuals, just as many psychologists and licensed professional counselors have developed expertise in family therapy. Clinical social workers have been at the forefront of the brief therapy movement and are often the best trained individuals in these therapies.

It may seem that we have ended up with a mental health system that, literally, sends you to one individual for your medication needs, to another for individual counseling, and to yet another for concerns about your family as a unit. In many ways this is true. Treatment can seem to be disjointed.

No single mental health practitioner can address all of your concerns, however, just as no single medical practitioner can address all of the body's needs. In trying to decide which practitioner to see, it is vitally important to think clearly about the underlying causes of your child's depression and to be totally honest with your child's pediatrician or family practitioner when asking for a referral to a mental health specialist. Honesty and clarity will help your doctor make the decision that is in your child's best interest.

INPATIENT TREATMENT

Your child's physician will probably use an informal decision tree in deciding who to refer you to. You should use one in your own thinking. For example, if your child is threatening suicide, threatening to harm others, or hearing intrusive voices that are telling her to harm herself or others, and if she is feeling like she cannot resist these impulses, inpatient treatment is necessary. This is available at either a freestanding psychiatric hospital or at a large hospital with a psychiatric unit. The typical procedure at an inpatient unit is for your child to receive a range of services from all of the practitioners we have mentioned. She will see a psychiatrist who will supervise her treatment, prescribe medications, and determine when it is safe to discharge her. She is likely to see a psychologist for testing and evaluation while hospitalized. The psychologist's report will identify both short-term and long-term concerns that affect her functioning and need to be addressed in her ongoing therapy. She will probably see either a psychologist or a clinical social worker for individual therapy and may also be in group therapy led by these same individuals. She is also likely to spend much time in less structured counseling interactions with the nursing staff, as well as with the unit's allied professionals, such as occupational therapists, recreational therapists, physical therapists, and so on. Most psychiatric units will make suggestions regarding outpatient psychiatrists and mental health counselors your child should see after hospitalization.

You should understand that hospitalization can have a powerful emotional effect upon children. While it helps to stabilize them, once home many develop a sense of shame or guilt over having been hospitalized. They begin to think of themselves as crazy or somehow damaged, which can lead right back to depression and self-concept concerns. This should be addressed in counseling. It is best to continue with outpatient counseling immediately after a hospital discharge so that the issues brought to light in the hospitalization can continue to receive attention.

Another word about hospitalization: Be prepared to be shocked by just how brief it will be. Years ago the public complained about how long hospital units or residential programs would keep kids. Today it is just the opposite. It is now routine for a suicidal child to stay in the hospital for five days or less. I know of stays of three days, although I do not know of anyone in the mental health professions who will say with any conviction that this is sufficient. My own belief is that any stay of less than two weeks serves only to divert the child and leaves insufficient time for getting down to the actual issues behind the suicidal thinking. For the first month after discharge from the hospital, suicidal children should be seen at least twice weekly in individual outpatient counseling and at least once weekly for family therapy. Such decisions are being driven entirely by the insurance companies, however, and the frequency of visits that I recommend are not likely to be covered by insurance.

OUTPATIENT TREATMENT

If you are asking your doctor for a referral for mental health services, but one that does not require inpatient hospitalizations, there are still a number of issues to be addressed. Your doctor should offer you guidance on whether or not it appears that medication will be useful or necessary for your child. Many pediatricians and family practitioners have sought out training in medications for mental health problems and may choose to prescribe these themselves. Many prefer to leave this to psychiatrists. In any case, it is unlikely that medication alone will be the recommended treatment.

If it strikes you or your doctor that the actual cause of your child's problem is within your family system, such as alcoholism, high levels of tension between the parents, neglect or abuse, then your doctor will be wise to refer you to someone with background and expertise in family therapy. If your family is functioning well in general and your child or teenager is struggling with an individual problem, then you will likely be referred to someone who specializes in individual psychotherapy. I should admit my own bias as a psychologist: I believe that the best therapy is one that heavily engages the parent in the work with the child or teenager. A good therapist has many tricks and insights to pass along to parents, so that they can continue to work with their child or teenager be-tween sessions. Children and adolescents will frequently present a distorted picture of their family and how it functions. Close contact with the family allows the therapist to observe how the family members interact. While I am a believer in traditional individual therapy, I have little trust in therapists who only want to work with your child behind closed doors and never bring you into the process.

EVALUATING THE TREATMENT

Bottom line, the thing you want to look for in your choice of a psy-chiatrist and your choice of a mental health therapist is the match between the practitioner and your child. Not every practitioner will match with every child. Competent practitioners will be will-ing to admit this when it happens and will refer you on to someone else. Keep in mind that this does not mean that the therapist failed or that therapy does not work. All it means is that the match was not quite right. It is sort of like the old saying, "If at first you don't succeed, try, try again." This holds particularly true in finding the right help for depressed children and teenagers.

There is little agreement on how to measure whether or not treatment is working. Insurance carriers ask mental health practi-tioners to write out their goals for treatment in measurable terms, much as you might expect a cardiologist to be able to give you some objective evidence that blood flow to the heart has improved with treatment. It is somewhat more difficult to quantify whether or not mental health treatments are working. Again from my own perspective, the parent has to be the ultimate judge. Is your child comfortable with the therapist and are you seeing improvements in the symptoms and behaviors that precipitated treatment to begin with? If you are not seeing improvements at the pace you ex-pected, does your therapist make you comfortable enough to discuss this and do you find the answers convincing? If so, you are probably well matched with your therapist and should stay the course until your child is functioning at a level similar to his successful peers. This may take a month. It may also take a year. No honest therapist will attempt to give you a guaranteed time frame for completion, given the complexity of their work.

MEDICATIONS

Another question that invariably arises in the course of treating a child for depression is medication. I have met parents who have taken their child to see a psychiatrist because they were convinced that medication was the only course of treatment that was worth considering. Similarly, I have met parents who have taken their child to see a psychologist because they were convinced that they did not want their child or teenager to depend on medication. I personally ask parents to take a pragmatic stance. If it becomes clearly possible to help a child escape depression through solely psychological means, then I see that as good. If psychological approaches do not work, but the child or teenager gets along just fine on medication, then I also see that as good. It is accepted practice in the mental health field to acknowledge that children and adolescents will benefit more from a combination of medication and psychotherapy than from either alone.

A full explanation of specific medications is beyond the scope of this book. The flow of new products to the marketplace is fast and makes books about medication rapidly become obsolete. In general, there are two classes of medications used for depression, these being tricyclic antidepressants, known generally in the field as tricyclics, and Selective Serotonin Reuptake Inhibitors, or SSRIs. There are also different medications used for treating other distinct disorders which fall within the depressive realm, such as Bipolar Disorder, also known as manic depression.

Medications have their opponents and their proponents. Suffice it to say that it is important to ask your prescribing doctor about the potential side effects of any medication and to ask your pharmacist to provide you with written material that describes in clear terms the potential problems associated with the medication. Many parents also find it interesting to go to the library and consult the *Physicians' Desk Reference* (the PDR), or a similar medication guide. Many public libraries carry reference guides to medications, as do most medical libraries at hospitals.

TEST YOUR CLINICAL JUDGMENT

Now we attempt to put all of what we have learned thus far to use. We will examine three different scenarios, and make decisions on how to proceed in each.

Test Case #1

Mandy is a high school junior. Her mother initially took her to see her pediatrician because she was unduly moody. She was angry and difficult to be around. Her pediatrician ran the standard medical tests, and on finding her to be physically healthy, referred her to me.

Her major clinical issues were that she argued with everything anyone said, spent much of her free time sleeping, and admitted to using alcohol and marijuana every weekend. She was very bright but was doing quite poorly in school. Her mother noted that Mandy had lost a noticeable amount of weight in the past six months and that she ate little other than crackers. She had taken on a Goth lifestyle, the hallmarks of which were wearing all black and adopting a fatalistic attitude about the world and about the future. Her best friend was a young man who claimed to be a vampire.

Mandy expressed an interest in most things related to death

and told me that she thought it would be "cool" to die. At the same time, she denied having any real urges to kill herself and did not spend any time thinking about ways to harm herself or others. She had no idea what type of career or lifestyle she wanted, and she denied finding anything interesting. The single exception to this, and the only aspect about her that made her seem like a normal teenager, was that she had a secret crush on a young man who hung out at the same coffee house she went to on weekends. He paid little attention to her, however. While it seemed apparent to me that she felt rejected, she denied these feelings. She denied having feelings of any sort.

What can we do to help? Go back to the ground rules that we talked about early in chapter 1. If you recall, in order to help a child escape depression, you have to take a critical look at the structural aspects of the child's or teenager's life, examine the types of things she thinks about and believes about herself and her life, and ask if her problems have a biological component.

Before you read any further, ask yourself what you are already thinking about Mandy's family structure, how she thinks, and whether or not medications might be useful. Put together a brief plan in your mind of how you would proceed were she your daughter.

It struck me that structural aspects of Mandy's life were pretty solid in some ways, but actually too loose in others. She had supportive parents who were accepting of her artistic personality. They gave her broad leeway to say and do as she pleased. Mandy was highly critical of her mother, although I have to admit that her mother was an anxious individual, not particularly enjoyable to be around because of her constant worrying.

After getting to know the family, I developed the opinion that Mandy was being given too much leeway in such decisions as whether or not to do homework, how late to stay out with her coffee shop friends, how to interact with adults, and so on. I told her parents that Mandy was failing to become an enjoyable person to be around and that I could see no reason for them to tolerate her angry, snippy comments. I asked them to remind her that while she was very bright and capable, she was failing to live up to her capabilities academically and socially. While her parents were initially hesitant, they finally did agree with me that Mandy would have to lose large amounts of her freedom if she did not work hard to change all of these problems.

It was not difficult to find out whether or not Mandy's thinking process had been distorted with hopeless beliefs. She was outspoken and liked to talk in a broad, negative sweep about the world. In general she found every potential teenager activity I could mention to be "boring," and she believed that life would always be boring to her (nothing will ever change). However, she did not seem to believe a lot of the other hopeless beliefs that we have discussed throughout this book. She didn't want to die, and she denied feeling like she was "not good enough." She did not believe that she had to be perfect and did not seem to use her mistakes as proof of something bad about her. The fact that the boy at the coffee house paid little attention to her did make her question her attractiveness. I was also of the opinion that her use of drugs and alcohol every weekend was having a depressing effect on her mood, her energy level, and her intellectual achievement.

Once you begin to summarize Mandy's life in this way, her treatment needs become much more apparent. Again, ask yourself what course of action you would take. My own course included scheduling sporadic but ongoing meetings with her parents to talk about how well they were doing in reestablishing themselves as the authority figures in their own home. While it angered her that they would have the temerity to tell her how she should live and how she should act, she did begin to moderate her negative, unpleasant behavior toward her parents. They got her attention by making sure that she understood clearly that as the parents, they

owned everything in the house, and she could say good-bye to access to all of it should she fail to become more pleasant to be
around.

I also had her schedule a series of meetings with a counselor
who specialized in drug and alcohol use. Mandy was one of those
teenagers who believe that there can be no fun without drugs or alcohol. She found people who did not use substances to be boring,
and she said that doing the usual teenager weekend activities without being in an altered state was boring. It became evident that she
was much more substance dependent than her parents realized.
Her counselor leaned on her to attend NA (Narcotics Anonymous)
meetings for teenagers, which she did.

I also referred her to a child psychiatrist for a medication evaluation. I was worried by the fact that her sleep cycle was being affected, and I was bothered by her weight loss and by her inability
to enjoy events that were once enjoyable to her or that most people would describe as enjoyable. These are all strong signs of depression. While it was certainly possible that talk therapy would
help with these issues, it was in her best interest to see if medications could help boost her out of her depressed mood more quickly
than would be the case with psychotherapy alone. Her psychiatrist
agreed that she was depressed, and prescribed antidepressant medication.

I also scheduled a series of weekly meetings with her. My own
agenda was to talk to her about how she was thinking, about how
she viewed her life, other people, the world, and so on.

Her agenda was to remain tight-lipped about herself once she
realized that my mission was to attempt to modify how she
thought. As is often the case, the early weeks of my contact with
her involved simply being in the same room with her and talking
about any number of surface issues. While it might be difficult for
an outsider to see the progress in this, the truth was that we were
establishing our therapeutic relationship. She was learning, slowly

but surely, that I was safe to be around and that I had a true interest in learning about how she thought. I made it clear that because I could understand her viewpoint, such as believing that nothing would ever change, this did not mean that I necessarily agreed with it. I also let her know that my intent was not to attack her beliefs. My intent was to help her determine if any of her beliefs were causing her to be depressed or causing her to behave in a manner that led to depression.

As we moved further into our contact, the real issues began to emerge. She had actually been quite smitten by the young man at the coffee house and had fallen head over heels in love with him. The fact that he seemed to have no interest in her struck a heavy blow, and she fell into a lifestyle of taking out her anger on others, her family in particular. His lack of interest in her brought out every conceivable insecurity: I'm not pretty enough. I'm not sexy enough. I'm not something enough, because if I were, he would notice. The words "I'm not" seemed to be at the front of every sentence she spoke about herself after she began to admit to what she was feeling. This made it clear that she found herself to be lacking.

Mandy had begun to define her self-worth by whether or not this young man noticed her. I began to ask her if it was true that no other young men paid attention to her. She had to admit that they did, but she also said that she found them to be boring. I asked her if it was actually true that these other young men were boring or if she was just not interested in them. She admitted that they were actually nice enough, just not her type.

Our work was proceeding slowly. She was able to understand my position that she had no actual proof of not being attractive enough. In reality, several young men were trying to get her attention, and they sounded to be desirable young men in the teenager dating scene. She had to admit that this meant something about her own desirability.

Then she made a fortuitous discovery. The young man she was interested in was gay. It turned out, in fact, that he was actually interested in Mandy's friend who claimed to be a vampire. The vampire, not being gay, was not interested in him.

This discovery opened up some avenues of discussion. Mandy came to a much better awareness that she had been trapped in "I can't live without this person" thinking. She also came to understand that she was basing her worth on the opinion of someone who was not genetically or psychologically disposed to be interested in her to begin with. She had been beating herself up over nothing, thinking he paid no attention to her because he found her unattractive.

His rejection had exposed the part of her that was the most insecure. While she pretended to reject the traditional female desire to be found attractive by others, it was in fact her looks and her desirability that she was most worried about.

Realizing just how insecure she was helped us to make sense of why, in her mother's words, she acted so "evil" half the time. Mandy protected herself through the concept that the best defense is a good offense. Her aggressive and hurtful comments were her shields. The only time I can remember her actually joking with me was one night when I told her that she was in the Captain Kirk role. She recognized that I was talking about the character from the television show "Star Trek," but she didn't know what I was getting at. "Same thing Kirk does when he's under attack," I told her. He turns to his helmsman and says, "Shields up!"

How does Mandy's story turn out? I had contact with her until she left for college, which in and of itself seemed to indicate that she had begun to reconsider the idea that she had no future. She continued to show indications of believing that her thoughts and beliefs were somehow superior to those of others, and it was not easy for her to just relax and be enjoyable to be around. She is likely to always have an edge to her and will only feel like she is in her own element when interacting with other edgy, artistic individuals.

She did manage to understand that the angry comments she made to her parents were inappropriate and served only to disturb the peace at home. She grudgingly admitted that her parents had the right to withhold transportation, money, major reinforcers (TV, telephone, CD player, long hot showers, snack foods), and freedom if she failed to make herself more enjoyable to be around. While she hated the idea of conforming to societal pressure, she also had to admit that unless her grades improved, there was little chance of her ever having the type of lifestyle she wanted. The medication she was taking seemed to have a beneficial effect on her appetite, and she made fewer statements about feeling depressed. I actually talked her into using power walking for both exercise and the benefit it could have on her mood. But I still secretly wonder if she power walked in an all black outfit.

Test Case #2

Troy is a boy who was nine when his father died mysteriously. He was found hanging from a doorknob. It was unknown if he had actually intended to kill himself or if he was experimenting with the sexual thrill that some people report from strangulation. Troy had been very close to his father. An only child, he had accompanied his father everywhere from the time he was still an infant. This was due in part to the fact that Troy's mother had abandoned the family early in his life, had simply run away to another state and started a new life for herself.

Troy's father took him everywhere also because Troy did not get along well with his stepmother. He had remarried when Troy was five. As Troy explained it to me, he never wanted his stepmother to think that she could take the place of his biological mother, even though his contact with her was limited to the sporadic phone call. Like many children, he harbored fantasies of getting his mother and father back together, even though the reality was that his father had remarried. When I asked him about this, he admitted that he was often purposefully mean to his stepmother, whom he referred to as his "stepmonster," in hopes that she would get tired of him and leave. His plan was to create a spot for his biological mother to return to.

Here's the summary: His father, who had loved him with notable intensity, was suddenly dead. His real mother, whom he pined for, was miles away and emotionally unavailable. He had managed to be so mean to his stepmonster that she had come to genuinely dislike him. And here's the part that makes his story really intriguing: He told me that his dead father came and stood by the foot of his bed every night. It was not frightening, he said. He said that he enjoyed it.

Troy had been referred to me by his school counselor. He had stopped doing homework and had begun to put his head on his desk and go to sleep in class. While he still hung out with his same friends at school, he was noticeably more silent and did not seem to enjoy the games and sports that he used to enjoy playing with his friends. At home he was quiet and uncommunicative. His stepmother, who was actually trying to be nice to him, had become embroiled in a legal battle with his biological mother. The battle was not over the biological mother trying to get custody of him. The battle was over the biological mother trying to get custody of his father's estate. Troy's father had left him and his stepmother quite rich.

Pause for a moment and begin to put his case together. What problems might Troy be experiencing that are related to how he is thinking and what he is believing? What problems might he have that are related to his family structure? Is it likely that his quietness and withdrawn behavior have a biological cause?

In the case of Troy, I quickly discounted the possibility that his psychological state had a biological cause or that it required medication to treat. Yes, he was withdrawn and sad. Yes, he was angry. If you have ever lost a parent as a youngster, you will understand all too clearly that this makes you angry at everything and everyone. When you lose someone you love, it makes you feel like there is a hole in the air, an empty space where that person used to be. The hole closes up with time, but you will not feel better until it closes. Troy had strong feelings of abandonment. From his perspective he had been abandoned both by his mother and now by his father.

My impression was that Troy was at risk of developing what I earlier described as the hole in the middle of the soul, that feeling of profound emptiness that comes when you have been forced to contend with too much aloneness too early in life. In talking with him I also found out that he believed many of the things that children secretly believe about parents running away and parents dying. He admitted to me that sometimes he believed that if he were a better kid, his biological mother would come back. At other times he said he believed that she would never come back and never reestablish contact with him. Nothing would change. He said he thought maybe she had run away because he cried too much as a baby or made too many messes. While he did not know about the particulars of his father's death, he thought that bad things, like the loss of his father, happened to bad people. He also had a strong sense of shame, telling me that he was the only kid in his class whose father had died. This made him feel different.

You can see that a world of hopeless beliefs were swimming around in his head, causing him to feel bad. We had to talk about each of them. For example, one of the first things we talked about was the idea that his father's death did not have anything to do with him or with his goodness as a child. He accepted his stepmother's idea that sometimes God calls people to heaven before we're ready for them to go.

We talked at great length about the idea that his failure to be a perfect child had nothing to do with his mother running away and not maintaining contact with him. He was able, over time, to understand that his mother must have had something bothering her deep inside and that there was a chance that he might never know what it was. Every time we discussed this mystery I had to point out to him, "But it didn't have anything to do with you."

We also worked to help him understand that the situation of his mother being out of contact with him might never change. He began to understand that while this would make him sad, it had nothing to do with his worth as a human being.

I mentioned his sense of shame about his father being dead. Shame is a sense of sorrow or regret over what you are. Troy was saying that he had been made unacceptable due to his father's death. I talked to him about this, using the double-standard method of breaking apart his faulty logic. I let him know that my mother died when I was in my late teens, and I asked him if that meant that I wasn't as good as the other kids at my school whose mothers were still alive. He recoiled from my logic and insisted that such a thing was impossible. I then asked him how it could be that his father's death had left him being not as good as the other kids, when my mother's death could not do the same to me. He got my point.

There is no escaping the issue of him seeing the ghost of his father every night. I would have no more made an attempt to take this comforting image away from him than I would try to take away a doll from a lost child. In this case, in particular, it was not my role to attempt to bring him into some scientific truth about a supposed metaphysical event. Who am I to mess with someone's sense of safety? Who am I to tell him that his experience was not real?

Troy and I talked for a number of months. The loss of his father was hard on him. He did draw closer to his stepmother, and I was able to convince her that she could not take his angry comments toward her personally. He was a little boy, in pain and lash-ing out, and what he needed from her, and from all of the adults in his life, was to be held safely and told that everything would turn out all right.

She took my advice about getting him cuddled up on the couch with her when they watched television. She would scratch his head and give him deep-muscle back massages, which seemed to soothe him and make him less prone to lash out. She took the idea of being emotionally available to him quite seriously, and she worked hard to make him feel loved. I had explained to her all about the hole in the middle of the soul, and she understood that children who do not feel loved crash and burn, sooner or later, no matter how smart they are.

I'm not aware of how the lawsuit between his biological mother and his stepmother ever turned out. The saddest part of the story for me, personally, was that one night his father told him that he could not come back anymore. Troy told me that he sat on his bed and watched his father just sort of fade away. And then he was gone.

Test Case #3

Nat is an almost seventeen-year-old male who was referred to me through the juvenile court system. His mother called to tell me that she had visited him in the facility where he was locked up. He told her he was having thoughts about death. If he didn't get some help, he told her, he would probably kill himself. I agreed to interview and evaluate him and to write an opinion for the court regarding his need, or lack thereof, for treatment.

He had been arrested for going on a small crime spree with another boy. He and the boy broke into a string of houses, vandalized them, and stole whatever seemed to be portable and valuable. They sold what they had stolen to an undercover cop. Later they resisted arrest.

When I first met Nat, he was accompanied to my office by a

detention facility officer. He wore a prison-issue orange jumpsuit and thin prison sandals (so that he couldn't run away very easily if he managed to escape). He had a chain around his waist, and his handcuffs were hooked into the chain in a manner such that he could move his hands only a few inches away from his body. It would not have been possible for him to grab anyone, or, for that matter, to go to the bathroom. He wore manacles around his ankles, hooked together by a chain so that he could shuffle along but could not run.

His guard asked me if I wanted him to take off the handcuffs once he was in my office. I told him that I did, as I saw little reason for him to remain so totally bound while we talked. The guard would be sitting in the hallway outside of my office. My intuitions told me, however, that there was little concern for danger. It had to do with the nature of the eye contact he made with me when we first met. His face, with his short prison haircut, looked hard. But his eyes looked young and frightened.

Here is Nat's story: He told me that he was to have a court hearing in a few days, at which time the judge would decide what to do with him. He had already pleaded guilty to the charges against him and was being cooperative with the police. His lawyer had informed him that the judge had a range of options. He could be sent to a boot camp for teenagers. He could be sent to a long-term detention facility, essentially a jail, for juvenile offenders. He could be placed on probation for several years and ordered to undergo treatment.

He said that if he was sent to a long-term facility, it was unlikely that he would come out alive. He told me that he would try to kill anyone who attempted to sodomize him, as he had been raped in a previous detention. He said that if, or when, he killed someone, he would soon be killed himself. Given all of this, he preferred to just go ahead and kill himself now, rather than face the possibility of going to the long-term facility. It seemed to me that wherever our conversation turned, all roads led to suicide.

The report that I wrote highlighting Nat's results must have caught the judge's eye. The judge's decision was to release him to probation, on the provision that he continue in treatment. The judge said, explicitly, that he must continue in treatment with me.

My first impression, on learning that the judge had released him so that he could enter treatment with me, was, "Oh joy, just what I need." But, I also had to admit that there was something distinctly likable about Nat. He was much like a lot of sociopathic young men in that he could be very up front and honest about the length, breadth, and depth of his criminal history. While you would not want to run across him in a dark parking lot and you wouldn't want your daughter to go out with him, he was relatively harmless as long as he was in a controlled situation. I hoped to take advantage of the fact that he knew he had to be good and that he could be snatched off the street by the court in ten seconds if he blew it or did not cooperate with treatment. I wanted to use these pressures to see if he would let me inside.

This is essentially what I said to him at the end of our first therapy session, after he was out on probation: "I will believe you unless it becomes apparent that you are lying to me. I will write positive, but realistic reports to the court every month as long as I believe that you are trying. If you end up making a fool out of me, I will ask the court to drop on you like a ton of bricks."

"Fair enough," was his response.

I was surprised at how much more sympathetic I was toward him as I got to know him. For one thing, seeing him in jeans, sweatshirt, and tennis shoes instead of an orange prison jumpsuit made him seem much more like a regular teenager. A misguided teenager, but a teenager none the less. And a depressed one to boot. He told me that he had no energy, that all he wanted to do was sleep. His mother reported that he was cranky and unpleasant to be around.

He said that he hated his life, because he basically had no life. He was under house arrest, permitted out only for brief periods of time to walk around the block to get some exercise. He hated the fact that his parents would not believe a word he said. His mother was so angry at him that she told him, in front of me, "Don't talk to me unless you're bleeding or your hair is on fire." His girlfriend had deserted him, and the boys in the neighborhood that he used to hang out with had been banned from associating with him. The families who used to hire him to cut their grass or rake leaves no longer wanted him on their property. He found that adults who used to see him on the street or in stores and say "Hello" now just looked at him and shook their heads.

At first he wanted to blame how he felt on everyone else. He said that no one was being fair to him, no one gave him a chance. He talked about how people ought to treat him differently and about how they didn't have to be so rude. He spent most of his time bemoaning what it was like for him to be around the people in his life.

This is a good place to compare notes. Some of the things that you need to know about Nat in order to decide how you might proceed are that he has lived all of his life in a supportive home environment. The man that I refer to in his story as being his father is actually his stepfather. He has been on the scene ever since Nat was about four years old and has been attached and involved. His biological father has been out of the picture for years. This does not seem to be a huge issue in Nat's life, given how close he has been to his stepfather. He has a brother and a sister, both younger and doing well. He has an older brother who lives in another state, who is struggling with his career but doing well otherwise. They are a middle-class family, neither rich nor poor. Nat has experimented with drugs and has even sold them in shockingly large quantity, if he is to be believed. He has had several bouts of brief contact with the police and the juvenile court system, all related to shoplifting.

Here are my impressions: Nat has been depressed twice since I got to know him. The first time, when I initially met him, was because the court system had its collective thumb on him and he had no wiggle room left. Lots of antisocials get depressed once they are caught. His mood eased considerably when he realized that he would not be going to a long-term detention facility or back to another boot camp. In the initial phases of therapy, he turned angry and defensive. He would challenge his need to be in therapy sessions and say that he had better things to do. He blamed all of his troubles on others. I did not see him as needing medication at that point. Instead, I saw him as needing a huge dose of new ways to think and new understandings about living among others.

I pointed out to him one day that while he complained about what it was like for him to be around the other people in his life, he never seemed to talk about what it was like for them to be around him.

He tried the typical antisocial cop-out when I attempted to move him in this direction. "How would I know what they think?" he asked. "I'm not them."

I explained that it was downright foolish for people to be unaware of the impact that they had on others. I told him that it would place limits on him that he would never even know were there, because he would act in a certain way without knowing that it was offensive or bothersome, and then be confused about why people were upset with him.

I pointed out some of the particulars about what it was like for others to be around him. He lived in a small community, and everyone knew what he had done. Not only were people avoiding him, but they were avoiding his mother and father. His brother and sister were being teased in the neighborhood by the other children. His parents felt shamed by his actions and had lost face in the community. These consequences were all the direct result of his behavior.

Then there was also the question of the seven thousand dollars in legal bills the parents had hanging over their heads. He became enraged at me at one point because I asked him how he intended to pay his legal fees, court costs, and fines. He shouted that he did not have to pay them, his parents had to pay them. I told him that I disagreed. His parents had to pay them for now, but he had to pay his parents back. I told him that this meant working weekend jobs and summer jobs for as long as it might take. I told him that if he had not paid his parents back by the time he either graduated from high school or finished a general equivalency degree (a GED), then he would be expected to go to work full-time and pay them back rapidly. He could forget about buying cars and stereos and surfboards and computers until his legal fees were paid. I also pointed out to him that the fact that he thought his parents ought to pay for his crime spree with money that they made legally through sweat and hard work should tell him a lot about what it was like for others to be around him.

Nat is becoming depressed again, although I still do not see him as a candidate for medication. He has lived a life in which he has been on automatic pilot, responding to every whim and impulse with little thought to potential consequences or impact upon others. He is finally realizing that it has led to being shunned by the people who used to be his friends. He knows that he is the teenager that parents in his neighborhood talk about when they tell their kids who not to be like when they grow up.

I continue to tell Nat that he must learn to trust his depression. I tell him that it is there for a reason, that his brain is trying to tell him that he must make massive changes in the way he thinks and acts before he will ever truly feel better. Sometimes the message of depression is hard to hear, and sometimes we don't like what it is telling us. The fact that Nat is depressed is his one saving grace. Were he to be going on with his life happy as a clam regardless of all of the grief he has caused for everyone around him, then he would be just like all of the other sociopaths out there in the world.

Nat has started to use his intellect to think during his sessions, as opposed to using it to defend himself from me. He does not like what he sees. We are at that stage of therapy in which I am asking him to replace his old ways of thinking with new ways. As cool as it might have been to be so easily able to fool others in the past, it only means that in life he has become a liar. As easy as it was to steal from stores from the time he was twelve, it only means that he has become a thief. As easy as it has been to make money dealing drugs, it only means that he has become a drug dealer. Is this, I continue to ask him, eyeball-to-eyeball there in my office, who you dreamed of being when you were five?

I know that I confound Nat's head with questions, but I do it in an attempt to overpower his old mental program with new thoughts and new beliefs that will help him steer clear of bad decisions. Garbage in, garbage out, I say to him. Negative beliefs lead to faulty behavior.

I say to him, for example, to pretend that he is in a war and is being chased by an enemy patrol. He comes to a river and finds two canoes. One is empty, and one has a paddle in it. Which will he choose?

"Easy," he says. "The one with the paddle."

"What does the river in this story represent?" I ask. "And what is the importance of the paddle?"

Nat does not like to push his thinking below the surface. But he will, if I keep at him. "The river represents my life," he says. "I don't know about the paddle."

I tell him that the paddle represents his plan about what kind of man he is going to become. If he just floats down the river, he'll arrive somewhere, but he won't have any control over where it is. It may end up being a desirable place, it may not. He may end up on a snag and never get loose. With the paddle, at least he has a chance.

Evaluate Your Clinical Judgment

How does your thinking about each child's needs match up with mine? As I saw it, Mandy, our Goth artist, needed a wide range of help. I helped her parents to understand that as much as their desire to leave her on her own to teach her independence and responsibility was admirable, it had backfired on them. They had to reestablish themselves as the authority figures, heads of the household who could provide consequences when necessary. This required that the parents make definite changes in their parenting philosophy and practices.

Mandy also needed medication, as her depression was at times quite deep and beyond the reach of weekly psychotherapy alone. The psychotherapy that she did require was long-term in nature, not the brief type of therapy that insurance companies and HMOs find so fashionable today. It was not enough to just try to decrease her symptoms, we had to try to rearrange her view of the world, of others, and of herself. She had to learn to allow some new ideas to infiltrate her mental program, such as: It is important in the grand scheme of things that others find you enjoyable to be around. Just because you do not agree with someone does not mean that he is stupid. Your worth as an individual does not depend upon whether some boy finds you attractive.

Troy did not need medication. He needed support, nurturing, holding, and loving. His situation was made more complicated by the fact that he had a strong yearning for a relationship with his biological mother, a yearning that was unlikely to ever be met. His stepmother stepped in admirably.

He had to change some of his beliefs. As I used to joke with him, we had to reprogram his meat computer. His new beliefs included accepting that he had nothing to do with his father's death and nothing to do with his mother's absence. He was not the cause of these bad things, and they did not happen because he was a bad boy. His main job, according to his new meat computer program, was to be a kid and have fun. His secondary job was to go to school and make his brain big. His third job was to help around the house. Any worrying was the job of the adults. He did not have to worry about being safe, because keeping him safe was his stepmother's job. He should expect little from his biological mother in the future, because that was exactly what she had given him in the past. He was not to take this personally because it was not his fault.

Nat got depressed for a bit once cornered by the court, felt better once he thought he could walk off scot-free, and got depressed again once he began to realize fully how he had been living his life and what he had caused others to think about him. He has yet to come to a point of needing medication because his depression is not threatening to his survival. Depression is threatening to his self-centered view of the world, and threatening to his impulsivity, and threatening to his relationships with other young thieves and scam artists. The main thing for him to understand is that he feels bad for a good reason and that he has to change.

Take the kind of thinking that you have done about Mandy, Troy, and Nat and apply it to your own child. Ask yourself if you believe medication, counseling, or family change might be useful and beneficial. If you suspect this is the case, approach your child's pediatrician or family practitioner about it, fully prepared to disclose everything you can about all of the forces affecting your child. Most important, think long and hard about what you hear your child saying, because this is the window you have onto what he is thinking about himself, others, and the world. Listen closely for evidence of the ten hopeless beliefs. Once you hear evidence of them, don't hesitate to talk.

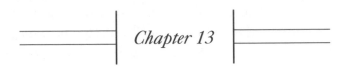

Chapter 13

Associated Disorders

Depression is a complicated enough subject all to itself. There are scientists and academics who devote entire careers to studying it, trying to find a cure or, short of that, trying to find ways to relieve its horrifying impact. To make matters even more complicated, depression can coexist with a number of other disorders, clouding not only the viewpoint and thinking of the sufferer, but clouding treatment strategies as well.

When you seek treatment for your child or adolescent, you want to make sure that the professionals helping you do a thorough diagnostic interview. You'll understand why as you read this chapter.

SUBTYPES OF DEPRESSION

There are several types of depressive disorders, each of which can have varying intensity, duration, and associations with other disorders. The criteria that we discussed in the introduction are the symptoms typically seen in what is known as Major Depressive Disorder. Its symptoms (depressed mood most of the day, diminished interest in pleasurable activities, thoughts of death, cranky mood) can hit a person hard and knock him flat on his back. With treatment his symptoms can be under control in a few months or so.

People who recover rapidly and do not experience symptoms again are described as suffering from Major Depressive Disorder, Single Episode. Unfortunately, all too often the symptoms ebb and flow, and the individual finds that he goes through episodes of Major Depression multiple times per year. This is referred to as Major Depression, Recurrent.

Dysthymic Disorder

While Major Depression can seem to come and go, there is also a variation that settles down around the person like a cloud. Dysthymic Disorder, as it is known, is characterized in children and adolescents as a period of at least one year in which the child is irritable, has appetite problems in which there is either weight loss or weight gain, sleeps too little or too much, has noticeable loss of energy, enjoys little, feels hopeless about life, feels confused, has trouble making decisions, and suffers from poor self-concept. Children going through dysthymia sometimes know that there is something wrong with the way they feel, but they keep it secret. Sometimes, dysthymic children are so used to feeling this way that, as amazing as it sounds, they come to believe that this is how everybody feels. These children and adolescents have great difficulty understanding why other people are happy, and they're often cynical and unbelieving about the idea that others truly do feel good.

Bipolar Disorder

Bipolar Disorder is a serious medical disorder requiring psychiatric treatment. The stereotypical public perception of Bipolar Disorder is that it is marked by periods of crashing depression, as seen in Major Depression, which over time evolve into periods of mania, a time in which the individual's thinking turns expansive and sometimes grandiose. Individuals in a manic phase of this illness often believe that they have discovered some secret that will save mankind. They may be mistaken as being psychotic because they bound from topic to topic, from one fantastic conclusion to another. Manic individuals often love the way they feel and will report having a sense of limitless energy and mental clarity that they do not want to give up. Because of this they resist treatment, especially in the manic phase.

There is much controversy among mental health professionals about the existence of Bipolar Disorder in children and adolescents. A decade ago you rarely heard about a teenager receiving this diagnosis. Today, you hear about it with increasing frequency in children who have yet to reach puberty. Its course is quite different than the symptoms for adults.

Bipolar children are often moody and explosive. Parents of bipolar children report that they feel like they are always walking on eggs when they are around them, as anything will set them off. Bipolar children and adolescents have little appreciation for the impact of their explosions on family members and friends. They clearly tend to blame their behavior on others.

I presently see several patients who have this disorder. One has been known, in fits of anger over issues everyone in his family describes as minor, to throw large rocks at his father's truck, turn over furniture, and punch holes in the wall. During one episode it took the majority of the local sheriff's office to corral him. This is amazing, considering he is twelve and weighs about one hundred pounds.

Another boy tends to melt down in the car over some innocuous comment and will begin to pound on his mother and spit on her while she is driving. One child I know got so mad about having to stop at a stoplight that he kicked the windshield out of the car.

Only the most hard-core believer in the power of psychotherapy or behavior modification will deny that bipolar children and teenagers need medication to help control themselves. The fact that these children truly cannot control themselves is a difficult admission for most parents. This seems to be the case, however. Once they are treated by a child psychiatrist with expertise in Bipolar Disorder, they frequently resume a much more peaceful coexistence with the world. Counseling is typically useful to help them come to grips with the fact that their behavior is not the fault of others and that they must continue with their medications in order to function at their best. Like bipolar adults, once they begin to feel better their first inclination is to stop taking their medication. "Why take it?" they'll ask. "I'm doing great."

Family therapy also helps parents and family members of a bipolar child or adolescent learn strategies to deal with him more effectively when he is on the edge. It is also vital that family members learn not to take the bipolar child's explosions personally and to be prepared to seek emergency services, such as hospitalization or intervention by legal authorities, if the bipolar individual begins to represent a realistic danger to himself or to others.

There are numerous subtypes of Bipolar Disorder, the description of which is beyond the scope of this book. Interested readers should consult the *Diagnostic and Statistical Manual of Mental Disorders* directly. It can be found at most libraries and in many bookstores. There are numerous other books available on Bipolar Disorder as well as on Major Depression. There are also numerous web sites on these disorders for the wired. As with all web sites, these should be read with a grain of salt, as anyone who pleases can publish his opinions.

Other Factors

There are yet other subtypes of depression. People can become depressed and suicidal due to medical conditions or injuries. It is not at all uncommon for children and adolescents to become depressed due to the onset of a disorder which requires medical attention. This can range from children being depressed once they begin to deal with acne and the impact it has on their appearance, to depression due to having to deal with diabetes, to depression secondary to major illnesses such as cancer.

Child and adolescent depression, as previously noted, is almost a given once substances enter the picture. From my perspective, the most prevalent form of depression in children and adolescents is what is known as Adjustment Disorder. An Adjustment Disorder is related to a known psychosocial stressor, such as too much tension in the home, a personal failure, academic difficulty, the breakup of a romantic relationship, or divorce. Depression related to these events typically will resolve itself within six months, unless the stressor is continuous, such as being picked on at school every day, having chronic academic difficulties, or chronic family problems. In such cases, Adjustment Disorder can roll over into Dysthymic Disorder.

Combined Disorders

It gets even more complicated. A child or adolescent, theoretically, can have a Dysthymic Disorder and a Bipolar Disorder at the same time. Each require different types of treatment. A dysthymic child or adolescent can also be highly perfectionistic or anxious. His inability to control his anger when he cannot do things perfectly or his tendency to explode when faced with the unknown or with unexpected events or transitions can sometimes mistakenly lead to a diagnosis of Bipolar Disorder when a diagnosis from the anxiety spectrum would be more appropriate.

Since writing the book, *The Defiant Child*, I have seen a lot of children and adolescents who display oppositional and defiant behavior. It is relatively rare for oppositional, defiant children to experience serious depression. They are cut from a different cloth. The exception to this rule, however, is the type of depression that happens to them when they are caught and placed under high levels of control by their parents or by other authorities. They can then become quite depressed. But for them, once the control has been lifted, depression tends to go "poof!"

At my office, I often see a reverse form of oppositional, defiant behavior. Parents will come in with a child or adolescent who is tearing it up pretty good at home or at school. Often someone has diagnosed Oppositional Defiant Disorder, and the parents have tried all of the methods talked about in *The Defiant Child* to no avail. They tell me that no punishment works on their child and that their child will wait them out.

While this ability to wait the parent out is sometimes a facet of the oppositional child's personality, I believe that more often it is related to depression. It makes perfect sense once you think about it. I used to joke with depressed adults that after the nuclear holocaust, two types of life forms would emerge from beneath the rubble. There would be cockroaches, because nothing can kill cockroaches. And there would be depressed people. Depressed people often expect nothing from the world and thus learn to absorb the blows. While they are lousy at having fun, they are great at accepting failure and adversity because that is how they expect things to go.

Children and adolescents who think this way should not be subjected to high levels of punishment when they are angry and acting out. Their anger and behavior is an expression of their depression. It is unlikely to change until the forces driving the depression are addressed. Most often, these forces revolve around self-hatred or high levels of self-criticism and self-rejection. They have taken themselves to court and found themselves guilty. They use their failures or mistakes as proof that they are no good, and they punish themselves thoroughly for their lack of worth or ability. Their behavior is the observable expression of what they are feeling inside.

ADHD AND DEPRESSION

Another group of children and teenagers who are prone to depression are those who have Attention Deficit Hyperactivity Disorder (ADHD). These children tend to be bright. They also tend to process information best when it is presented to them in a visual format or through hands-on learning. Too often they find themselves in classrooms in which they are expected to sit still and listen, to take it all in through the ear, which is their weakness to begin with. They get in trouble because they can't sit still, or they know they are smart but have trouble getting themselves organized enough to do well on written tests and lengthy projects. They fail to live up to what they secretly know to be their ability level, and because of this they begin to doubt themselves. This is when depression sets in. They are best treated by someone who has a deep understanding of both ADHD and depression. As their depression appears to reside in their self-concept, my preference is to treat their depression through cognitive therapy, as opposed to medications.

I will limit my comments to using stimulant medication for ADHD to indicating that for many children, it is a godsend. While controversy rages about it, and while there are realistic worries about its long-term effects, many children blossom when they use it. My general advice for the parents of children who are diagnosed with ADHD is to suggest that they try stimulants and educate themselves thoroughly on methods of behavior modification. In many cases they will see a night-and-day difference just from the stimulants. If the difference is not clear and dramatic, rely on the behavioral techniques as best as possible.

LEARNING DISABILITIES AND DEPRESSION

A second group that goes down a similar path are children and adolescents with learning disabilities. The term "learning disability" is the most maligned term in the whole of the English language, as far as I'm concerned. These are often children who are quite bright when measured on their ability to do real-world tasks, but who have some glitch in the way that their brain processes certain types of information. For example, they may be able to tell you all kinds of facts about the solar system, but be totally unable to write any of it down in an coherent fashion. They may be able to rebuild an engine, but not write a paragraph. They may have difficulties limited to very specific areas, such as reading, working math problems, or learning a foreign language. In any case, they are often thought of as being "stupid" or "dumb" by their classmates because of their learning disability. Too often they begin to believe in this assessment, and this is when depression sets in.

Again, the treatment of choice is with a counselor or therapist who has a deep understanding of learning disabilities and depression. Medication should be used only if the child's depression reaches the point of total academic failure or self-harm.

• • •

Depression is associated with any number of other psychological conditions that come to the attention of child and adolescent mental health practitioners. I've yet to meet a happy anorexic or bulimic individual. Children with tic disorders, such as Tourette's Syndrome, are frequently depressed due to being ashamed of their involuntary noises and body movements. Children who can't sleep often have undiagnosed depression. Children and teenagers who pull out their own hair (Trichotillomania) get depressed due to the rude questions others ask about them being bald.

The list could go on and on, which returns me to the point brought up at the beginning of this chapter: Depression is a complex issue. When you seek treatment for your child or teenager, make sure you do it with someone who has strong interest and expertise in the subject. Mental health professionals are like all other doctors in that regard. I once knew a cardiologist who told me jokingly that his field of interest and expertise extended from "here to here." He held a finger on one hand to the middle of his collar bone, and a finger on his other hand to the tip of his sternum. Some mental health professionals can't stop thinking about anxiety, or eating disorders, or schizophrenia, such is their interest in a specific subject matter. Be sure you find someone who is, as odd as it may sound, passionate about depression.

Afterword

A Few Kind Words about Depression

I can't help but write personally about depression. I've worked with so many of these children and teenagers over the years, seen so many of them come close to stepping over into oblivion or living a life numbed by self-rejection or hopelessness, that depression has become something of a crusade for me.

My late-night musings about the children and adolescents I read about who have killed themselves are often guided by the notion of therapy being akin to reprogramming a computer. How do we face the hopeless beliefs that can cause death and work backwards through their roots and origins until we find that place where the child felt whole so we can return him there?

Any child or adolescent who has committed suicide has probably gone through torturous pain for weeks and months before his death. He probably managed to hide what he was thinking and feeling about his life. I ask myself, what if someone had been able to help the boy in my neighborhood who shot himself last summer learn to think about himself and his life in a different way, in a way that might have stopped him at the last moment?

In my ruminations about this boy's death, it is just like Kurt Vonnegut envisioned throwing time into reverse in *Slaughterhouse Five,* thereby saving thousands of people from the firebombing of Dresden during World War II. The bullet that killed the boy freezes in midair then, magically, recedes back into the gun barrel, pushing smoke and fire back down the throat of the weapon. The boy stands up and walks backwards down the hallway into his parents' bedroom and returns the gun to the closet shelf, placing it under the sweaters where it had been hidden. He walks backwards down the stairs and out the door, backwards all the way to the bus stop, where he leaps backwards up onto the first step. The bus, driving in reverse, returns to school, where he thumbs backwards through books and makes writing disappear into the tip of his pencil as it moves from right to left across his notebook paper. Back we continue to go in time, to the point where self-hatred and fear and loss of hope began their insidious processes, and at that point we do our best to give this boy a new way to think.

Fortunately, most children and adolescents who get depressed don't commit suicide. This should not numb us to the prospect of what it would be like to lead a life in which everything felt gray and flat and lifeless, the landscape inhabited by depressed children and adolescents.

I do not mean for us to embrace depression in any strange way. We should treat it as we would any messenger riding toward us from the side of the enemy. We ignore it at our own peril. All of us, as parents, should make sure that we begin to ask our children how they feel about themselves in general, how they are thinking about themselves when they are encountering difficulty in academics, or sports, or socially. You may be surprised about how much your child or adolescent will reveal, if you just ask.

As the parent, you cannot know what types of thinking and self-reflection your child needs help with if you fail to ask. It is in this regard that we must be thankful when a depression is strong enough to get our attention. It is giving us a clear signal that something is amiss with our child, instead of placing us later in that painful situation of wishing we had only known.

Index

emotional pain in, 44
home environment impact on,
44–45, 98
Joe (case study), 98–99
as miniature marriage, 97, 98
parental role in managing adolescent, 105
replacement beliefs used for handling, 105–106
stress caused by, 126
suicide threats in, 40–42, 101,
102
technology impact on, 100
Replacement beliefs
for controlling stress, 130–131
for controlling substance abuse,
114–115
for ending suicidal thoughts, 55
for escaping hopelessness,
140–141
for handling fairness issues, 96
for handling relationships,
105–106
for replacing fear of mistakes, 74
for replacing fear of rejection, 85
for replacing negative beliefs,
36–37
for replacing self-hatred, 64
Resistance, depressed children and,
32–33, 34
Rules and regulations
handling depression by setting,
10–13
self-hatred concept and, 62

Schizophrenia, childhood, 127
Selective Serotonin Reuptake Inhibitors (SSRI's), 152

Self-doubt, lack of parental love and,
117, 118
Self-hatred
crazy people and, 62–63
defiant children and, 177
depression caused by, 56–57
replacement beliefs for replacing,
64
symptoms of, 63–64
using notion of proof for analyz-
ing, 57–60
Self-worth
hopelessness and, 133
Mandy (test case study), 153–159
Sex in miniature marriages, 104
Sexual abuse
Allison (case study), 15–16
stress caused by, 126
Shelby (case study), 110–111
Skunk training, fairness issues and,
89–91
Slaughterhouse Five, 182
Social skills
communication techniques and,
80–83
fear of rejection and, 78–79
Sociopaths, 91
Stimulants, treating ADHD with,
178
Stress
caused by academic pressures,
52–53
depression caused by, 3, 125–126
how to talk to child under, 32,
126–129
replacement beliefs for replacing,
130–131
seeking help for managing, 126
sources of, 126